Instant Pot™ Cookbook

550 Delicious Recipes for Everyday Cooking

By Meg Harper

All rights reserved. No part of this publication may be reproduced, distributed, or transmitted in any form or by any means, including photocopying, recording, or other electronic or mechanical methods, without the prior written permission of the publisher, except in the case of brief quotations embodied in critical reviews and certain other non-commercial uses permitted by copyright law.

Although the author and publisher have made every effort to ensure that the information in this book was correct at press time, the author and publisher do not assume and hereby disclaim any liability to any party for any loss, damage, or disruption caused by errors or omissions, whether such errors or omissions result from negligence, accident, or any other cause.

Table of Contents

Instant Pot Breakfast Recipes

- Steel Cut Oats 12
- Hard Boiled Eggs 13
- Greek Yogurt Recipe 14
- Korean Style Steamed Eggs 16
- Eggs De Provence 17
- Poached Eggs with Potato Hash 18
- Banana French Toast 20
- Mini Omelets 22
- Coconut Yogurt 23
- Pumpkin Steel-Cut Oatmeal 24
- Buckwheat Porridge 25
- Blueberry Jam 26
- Apple Squash Porridge 27
- Banana Bread 28
- Spanish Tortilla 29
- Almond Milk Yogurt 31
- Steamed Eggs 32
- Blueberry Breakfast 33
- Potatoes Casserole 34
- Egg Casserole 35
- Breakfast Burrito Casserole 36
- Veggie Quiche 37
- Peaches and Cream 38
- Chocolate Chip Bread Pudding 39
- Breakfast Cobbler 40
- Breakfast Porridge 41

Instant Pot Dinner Recipes

- Red Beans and Rice 42
- Teriyaki Turkey Meatballs 44
- Beef Gyros 46

Paleo Beef Barbacoa 48

Buffalo Chicken Meatballs 49

Shepherd's Pie 51

Beef Stroganoff 52

Mac n' Cheese 54

Asian Ramen Noodles 55

Delicious Chili 56

Pulled Chicken 58

Chipotle Barbacoa 59

Apple Cider Pork Loin 60

Delicious Chicken 61

Ranch Pot Roast 62

Zuppa Toscana 63

Chicken Enchiladas 64

Swedish Meatballs 65

Steak Tacos 66

Baby Carrots with Mint 67

Chicken Fettuccini Alfredo 68

PIZZA PASTA 70

Ricotta 71

Instant Pot Dessert Recipes

Pumpkin Chocolate Bundt Cake 72

Mini Lava Cake 74

Red Velvet Lava Cake 75

Chocolate Cheesecake 77

Orange Marmalade 79

Apple Crisp 80

Salted Caramel Cheesecake 81

Applesauce 83

Mini-Lemon Cheesecakes 84

Oreo Cheesecake 86

Banana Chocolate Bundt Cake 88

Blueberry Pudding 90

Peanut Butter Cheesecake ... 92
Samoa Cheesecake ... 93
Apple Upside-Down Cake ... 95
Chocolate Cake ... 97
Pumpkin Pudding ... 98
Chocolate Pudding Cake ... 100
Chocolate Lava Cake ... 101
Peppermint Cheesecake ... 103
Greek Yogurt Cheesecake ... 105
Maple Flan ... 106
Lavender Crème Brûlée ... 108
Bread Pudding ... 109
Chocolate Zucchini Bites ... 110

Instant Pot Chicken Recipes

Lemongrass and Coconut Chicken ... 112
Lemon Mustard Chicken and Potatoes ... 114
Chicken Cacciatore Recipe ... 115
Moana Shredded Chicken ... 117
Creamy Chicken Alfredo Pasta ... 119
Chicken, Mushrooms and Artichoke Hearts ... 121
Salsa Shredded Chicken ... 122
Sticky Chicken ... 123
Polynesian Chicken ... 125
Honey Bourbon Chicken ... 127
Rotisserie Chicken ... 128
Buttery Lemon Chicken ... 130
Chicken Breasts ... 132
Chicken Taco Bowls ... 133
Honey Sesame Chicken ... 134
Chicken Burrito Bowls ... 136
Chicken Teriyaki ... 137
Herbed Chicken ... 139
Thai Chicken ... 141

Delicious Shredded Chicken ... 142

General Tso's Chicken ... 143

Apricot Chicken ... 145

Delicious Chicken and Rice ... 146

Whole Chicken ... 148

Thai Peanut Chicken & Noodles ... 149

Instant Pot Pork Recipes

Chinese Pork Tenderloin ... 150

Bbq Pulled Pork ... 152

Kalua Pig ... 154

Pork Chops, Rice and Vegetables ... 156

Honey Pork Chops ... 157

Balsamic Pork Tenderloin ... 158

Boneless Pork Chops ... 159

Mexican Pulled Pork ... 160

Maple Pork Stew ... 161

Hawaiian Pork ... 163

Jamaican Pork Roast ... 164

Sweet Glazed Pork Loin ... 165

Pork Tenderloin ... 167

Chile Pork Stew ... 168

Pork Chops with Rice ... 169

Pork Tenderloin with Rosemary ... 170

Pork Adobo ... 172

Peach Pork ... 173

Pork Chops with Apples ... 174

Teriyaki Pork Loin ... 175

Goan Pork Vindaloo ... 176

Braised Pork with Potatoes ... 178

Shrimp and Pork Dumplings ... 180

Pulled Pork with Cranberries ... 182

Keto Pork Meatball Bites ... 183

Instant Pot Beef Recipes

Beef Burgundy...185

Salisbury Steak and Gravy...187

Beef and Broccoli..189

Shredded Beef...192

Taco Meat..194

Italian Beef..196

Beef Bbq Recipe..197

Hamburger Helper...199

Corned Beef and Cabbage...200

Smoked Brisket...201

Mexican Shredded Beef..202

Mediterranean Beef...206

Beef Lo Mein..208

Beef Vegetable Soup...210

Ground Beef Shawarma Rice..211

Delicious Beef Bourguignon...212

Beef and Macaroni..214

Hearty Beef Stew..216

Ground Beef Bulgogi..218

Indian Beef Curry..219

Corned Beef and Cabbage...221

Beef Pasta Soup...223

Beef Spaghetti...224

Instant Pot Side Dish Recipes

Stuffed Peppers...225

Five Minute Cheesy Sauce..227

Eggplant and Olive Spread..228

Crème Brûlée..230

Banana Bread..231

Sausage and Peppers...232

Pumpkin Puree..233

Pumpkin Butter 234

Potato Salad 235

Spaghetti Squash 236

Sweet Brussels Sprouts 237

Roasted Potatoes 238

Butternut Squash Risotto 239

Macaroni And Cheese 241

Cabbage and Turkey Sausage 242

Black Beans with Chorizo 243

Baked Beans 244

Spanish Rice 245

Pico De Gallo 246

Calrose Rice 247

Sticky Rice 248

Coconut Rice 249

Congee with Minced Beef 250

Cranberry Sauce 251

Basmati Rice 252

Instant Pot Soup Recipes

Chicken Tortellini Soup 253

Smoky Mexican Chicken Soup 254

Chicken Enchilada Soup 256

Beef Barley Soup 258

Broccoli and Potato Soup 260

Loaded Potato Soup 261

Chicken and Lentil Soup 262

Carrot Ginger Soup 263

Tortilla Soup 264

Lasagna Soup 265

Garden Harvest Soup 266

French Onion Soup 268

Navy Bean Soup 270

Minestrone Soup Recipe 272

Chard Stem Soup	274
Hearty Broccoli Soup	275
Italian Soup	277
Mexican Chicken Soup	278
Beef, Beans and Tomato Soup	279
Chunky Beef, Cabbage and Tomato Soup	280
Cheesy Cauliflower Potato Soup	282
Creamy Thai Coconut Chicken Soup	283
Tomato Basil Soup	284
Sausage, Kale, And Sweet Potato Soup	285
Tomato Soup with Roasted Tomatoes	287
Ham White Bean Soup	289
Chicken Meatball Kale Soup	290
Broccoli & Bacon Soup	292
Potato Soup with Cheddar And Leek	293
Beef and Beer Stew	294
Andouille Sausage Stew	296
Vegan Hoppin' John	297
Vegan Green Chile Stew	298
Apple Spice Beef Stew	300
Beef Luau Stew	301
Italian Sausage Stew	302
Beef and Garlic Stew	304
Korean Chicken Stew	306
Goat Stew	309
Chicken Pot Pie Stew	311
Beef and Butternut Squash Stew	312
Japanese Pork Tender Rib Stew	314
Kimchi Stew	316
Spicy Beef Stew	318
Chicken and Sweet Potato Stew	319
Mung Bean Stew	321
Italian Chickpea Stew	323

Veggie Stew 325

Chicken Stew 327

Instant Pot Healthy Recipes

Quinoa 329

Black Beans 330

Jasmine Rice 331

Potato Salad 332

Wild Rice Pilaf 334

Pinto Beans 335

Black Bean Soup 336

Black-Eyed Peas and Ham 337

Ham and Bean Soup 338

Beef Chili 339

Chicken Noodle Soup 341

Cilantro Lime Rice 342

Delicious Chicken Noodle Soup 343

Buffalo Chicken 345

Lentil Tortilla Soup 346

Squash Beef Stew 348

Greek Pork Pitas 350

Cauliflower Soup 351

Beef Drip Sandwiches 352

Chicken and Smoked Sausage Stew 353

Beef Chili 355

Onion Soup 357

Mexican Beef Stew 358

Oatmeal 359

Thai Coconut Chicken Soup 360

Brown Rice 362

Chicken Lettuce Wraps 363

Queso With Cauliflower 364

Sweet Potato Chili 366

Ham and Bean Soup 367

Steamed Asparagus 369

Pesto Chicken Rice Soup 370

Quinoa Porridge 371

Red Lentil Soup 372

Pot Roast 373

Steel Cut Oats

Total Time: 15 mins

Serving Amount: 4

INGREDIENTS

1 cup steel cut oats

3 cups water

DIRECTIONS

Pour steel cut oats in the steel pot.

Add 3 cups water.

Secure the lid, press manual, and set time to 3 minutes.

Allow the Instant Pot to come to pressure - approximately 5 minutes.

When finished, natural release pressure - approximately 5-10 minutes

Hard Boiled Eggs

Total Time: 10 mins

Servings: 1-2

INGREDIENTS

Pasture raised eggs

1 cup water

DIRECTIONS

Plug in your Instant Pot

Pour one cup water in the bottom of the stainless bowl

Place in a stainless strainer/steamer basket

Place your desired number of eggs on top of the opened steamer basket

Put the lid on

Power on and press the manual button

Adjust to 8 minutes on the display

Close and lock the lid and make sure the vent is closed

Quick release when done

Let cool and vent completely before opening lid

Greek Yogurt Recipe

Total Time: 10 hrs 5 mins

Servings: 14

INGREDIENTS

1 Gallon Milk (Whole, 2%, 1% or Fat Free)

2 Tablespoons Yogurt Starter

DIRECTIONS

Sterilize

Add three cups of water to the Instant Pot cooking pot, lock on lid and close Pressure Valve. Push the Steam button and adjust time to 5 minutes. When beep sounds, open Pressure Valve (Quick Release). When all pressure has been released, remove lid and dump out the water. Dry and cool off cooking pot.

Make Yogurt (Not Under Pressure)

Pour Milk into cold/cool Instant pot. Cover with IP Lid or Glass Lid. Close the Pressure Valve, if desired.

Push Yogurt button and then the Adjust button, until it says "boil." A few times during boil cycle, remove lid and whisk Milk.

When beep sounds, open lid, whisk and take temperature. If the temperature is not 180 degrees, repeat last step or use the Sauté/Low function to get it up to temp, whisking continuously.

When 180 degrees is reached, remove cooking pot and place in kitchen sink full of cold water. Cool Milk down to 95-110 degrees, whisking often.

Temper starter - scoop out some Milk and whisk in the Starter. Pour Milk (w/the Starter) back into cooking pot, whisk thoroughly.

Place cooking pot back into the Instant Pot and cover with IP Lid or Glass Lid. Press Yogurt button.

The display screen will say 8:00 (hit again or adjust, if necessary). Make sure display reads "Normal." Use the +/- button to adjust time to your desired level of tartness. The program will end after whatever time you have set to incubate.

When Cycle ends, remove cooking pot (covered) to refrigerator, until cool, 6-8 hours (undisturbed).

Make it Greek Yogurt

Use a Yogurt Strainer and strain the yogurt in the refrigerator for at least two hours. Your whey should be translucent/clear. If the whey is cloudy, add another layer of cheesecloth/butter muslin to your straining device. The Euro Strainer should produce clear whey.

Korean Style Steamed Eggs

Total Time: 110 mins

Servings: 1-2

INGREDIENTS

1 Large egg

1/3 Cup cold water

Chopped scallions

Pinch of sesame seeds

Pinch of garlic powder, salt and pepper

DIRECTIONS

Mix the egg and water in a small bowl

Strain the egg mixture over a fine mesh strainer into a heat proof bowl

Add the rest of the ingredients and mix well and set aside.

Add 1 Cup of water to the inner pot of Instant Pot

Place the trivet or steamer basket in the pot

Place the bowl with the egg mixture on the trivet or steamer basket.

Close the lid tightly and close the vent valve.

Press manual setting on HIGH and set the timer for 5 minutes.

When the timer goes off, perform a quick release.

Eggs De Provence

Total Time: 40 mins

Servings: 6

INGREDIENTS

6 eggs

1 small onion chopped

1 cup cooked ham or bacon

½ c heavy cream

1 c chopped kale leaves

1 c cheddar cheese1 tsp Herbs de Provence

1/3 tsp sea salt and pepper

DIRECTIONS

Whisk eggs with heavy cream

Add the rest of the ingredients and mix well.

Pour the mixture into a heat proof dish and cover.

Add one cup of water in the Instant pot

Place the trivet or steamer basket inside.

Close the lid tightly, close the vent valve

Press manual on high pressure for 20 minutes and perform a natural pressure release.

Poached Eggs with Potato Hash

Total Time: 25 mins

Servings: 2

INGREDIENTS

1 Cup of peeled, cubed potatoes

2 eggs

1 Tbsp cooked and chopped bacon

2 Tbsp bacon fat or grass-fed butter

1 sliced jalapeno pepper

½ Cup of diced onion

1 tbsp + chopped cilantro

1 tsp + Taco Seasoning

DIRECTIONS

Pour 1 cup of water in the inner pot and place the trivet inside.

Place the bowl with cubed potatoes on the trivet.

Close the lid tightly and close the vent valve.

Set Instant Pot on Manual for HIGH pressure for 2 minutes. Or you can cook the whole potatoes for 3 minutes and cut them afterwards.

Meanwhile, chop onions, bacon, jalapeno pepper and cilantro.

When timer goes off, perform a quick release

Press Cancel.

Take out the potatoes and set aside.

Remove the trivet and drain the water.

Set Instant Pot on "Sauté" and wait until the screen says, "Hot"

Add bacon fat or butter and sauté onions until translucent.

Add potatoes, bacon, pepper, cilantro and taco seasoning and mix well.

Pat down the potatoes to create a little crater in the middle.

Crack both eggs gently into the crater of the potato hash.

Close the lid tightly and close the vent valve.

Set on high pressure for 1 minute.

When timer goes off, perform a quick release.

Using a flexible spatula or a flat wooden spatula, lift the potato hash with the eggs on top, without breaking the egg yolk.

Banana French Toast

Total Time: 40 mins

Servings: 6-8

INGREDIENTS

5-6 slices of French bread, cubed

4 bananas, sliced

2 tablespoons brown sugar

¼ cup cream cheese

3 eggs

½ cup milk

1 tablespoon white sugar

1 teaspoon vanilla extract

½ teaspoon ground cinnamon

2 tablespoons chilled butter, sliced

¼ cup pecans, chopped

DIRECTIONS

Slice french bread into cubes.

Grease a 1½ QT round baking dish or cake pan for the 8 qt Instant Pot. If you have a smaller pressure cooking pot, use a baking dish that will fit inside of the pot.

Add a layer of bread to the bowl.

Layer one sliced banana over the bread, then sprinkle one tablespoon of brown sugar over the bananas.

In a microwave, melt the cream cheese 30-45 seconds until it's creamy enough to spread. Cover the bananas and bread with cream cheese.

Add the rest of the bread to the bowl and layer one more sliced banana over the bread.

Sprinkle one tablespoon of brown sugar over the bananas and half of the pecans over the top.

Place sliced butter pieces over the bread as the top layer.

In a mixing bowl, beat the eggs with a whisk. Whisk milk, white sugar, vanilla, and cinnamon into egg mixture.

Pour egg mixture over the bread, making sure to coat the bread well.

Pour ¾ cup water into the Instant pot and place a trivet or pot lifter in the bottom of the pot. If you don't have a trivet to lift the pan out of the hot Instant Pot, make a sling out of a large foil strip.

Center the pan on the trivet or foil strip and lower it into the Instant Pot.

Select the porridge button, and then add 5 minutes to the cook time.

Mini Omelets

Total Time: 10 mins

Servings: 2-4

INGREDIENTS

beaten eggs

cheese

Tastefully Simple Bacon

Onion

some leftover meat and vegetables

DIRECTIONS

Use the steamer basket and place the baking cups around the bottom and fill them with the filling.

Set the pot to manual and used the +/- buttons to select 10 minutes of pressure.

When the pressure cycle is complete, perform a quick pressure release and sprinkled shredded cheese on top. Put the lid back on for a couple of minutes to melt the cheese.

Coconut Yogurt

Total Time: 6-8 hrs

Servings: 2-4

INGREDIENTS

2 cans (1 L) coconut cream

1 package yogurt starter with live cultures

1 tbsp grass-fed gelatin

3 half pint jars and lids

Favorite toppings

DIRECTIONS

Put the coconut cream into the Instant Pot liner. Press Yogurt, and Adjust. This will bring it to a boil.

When the readout switches to Yogurt, remove the liner from the pot, turn off the Instant Pot.

Let the now liquid coconut cream cool, either on the counter or fridge so the temperature drops to below 100F, but not too cold (important).

Once the coconut milk is the right temperature, whisk in the starter a little at a time, no lumps.

Press the Yogurt button and adjust the time, the longer you set the timer, the tangier it will be. 8 hours is recommended.

While it is still warm, whisk in the gelatin a little at a time.

Pour equally into the jars leaving room for the desired toppings.

Put on the lid and refrigerate 4-6 hours.

Mix well before serving.

Pumpkin Steel-Cut Oatmeal

Total Time: 10 mins

Servings: 6-8

INGREDIENTS

4 ½ cups water

1 ½ cups steel-cut oats

1 ½ cups pumpkin puree

2 teaspoons cinnamon

teaspoon allspice

teaspoon vanilla

COFFEE CAKE TOPPING

½ cup coconut sugar or brown sugar

¼ cup pecans or walnuts, chopped

tablespoon cinnamon

DIRECTIONS

Add all the instant pot ingredients to your stainless-steel insert and put it into the base. Secure the lid and make sure the valve is closed. Set on manual and cook for 3 minutes.

While the oats are cooking, mix all the topping ingredients together and store in an airtight container.

Once the oats are cooked, allow the pressure to come down naturally. Once the silver pressure indicator goes down you can open the lid.

Buckwheat Porridge

Total Time: 10 mins

Servings: 3-4

INGREDIENTS

1 cup raw buckwheat groats

3 cups rice milk

1 banana, sliced

¼ cup raisins

1 tsp. ground cinnamon

½ tsp. vanilla

DIRECTIONS

Rinse buckwheat and place in Instant Pot.

Add rice milk, banana, raisins, cinnamon and vanilla and close lid.

Be sure the steam release is in the closed position and manually select 6 minutes high-pressure cooking time.

When timer beeps at the end of the cooking cycle, turn pot off and allow time for the natural release of pressure, about 20 minutes.

Once pressure is released, carefully open lid and stir porridge with a long-handled spoon.

Add more rice milk to individual servings to achieve preferred consistency.

Blueberry Jam

Total Time: 10 mins

Servings: 3-5 jars

INGREDIENTS

2 pounds blueberries, fresh or frozen

1-pound honey

DIRECTIONS

Add blueberries to inner pot of Instant Pot.

Pour in honey.

Put Instant Pot on low heat (Keep Warm function) until honey melts.

Stir occasionally.

When melted, turn Instant Pot to high heat (Sauté function) until honey boils.

When it boils, put the lid on.

Press the Cancel button, and then set to high for 2 minutes.

When cooking time is complete, hit the Cancel button to turn off the heat, and unplug.

Let depressurize naturally.

When depressurized, remove lid and turn Instant Pot back on to high heat (Sauté function).

Let boil until some of the water has evaporated off, and the jam is gelled when dripped off a spoon.

Store in the refrigerator.

Apple Squash Porridge

Total Time: 25 mins

Servings: 3

INGREDIENTS

4 small or 2 large apples unpeeled, flesh cut from the cores

1 delicata squash washed and whole

1/2 cup bone broth with little fat

3 Tablespoons slippery elm

2 Tablespoons gelatin

2 Tablespoons maple syrup

1/2 teaspoon cinnamon

1/8 teaspoon each: cloves and ginger

Pinch of sea salt

DIRECTIONS

Place whole, uncut delicata squash into insert pot. Add apple chunks. Add bone broth and spices. Make sure rubber ring is in place in the Instant Pot lid, and secure lid, closing steam valve. Choose Manual setting and 8 minutes.

When timer goes off, allow pressure to release naturally for 10 minutes; then press Cancel, place a dish towel over steam valve and open it to release any remaining pressure. Remove lid and insert, so the pot's contents begin to cool.

When cool enough to handle, place delicata on a plate or cutting board. Cut in half length-wise and remove seeds with spoon. (They come out very quickly and easily.) Place squash halves and pot's contents (apples, broth and spices) into blender.

Add remaining ingredients: optional slippery elm, gelatin, maple syrup and sea salt. Blend for about 30 seconds, until smooth. Serve with optional toppings, or pour into portable containers for packing in lunches.

Banana Bread

Total Time: 55 mins

Servings: 3

INGREDIENTS

7" spring form pan

4 mashed bananas

1 stick soft butter

1 tbsp. vanilla

2 eggs

½ cup sugar

2 cups flour

1 tsp baking powder

DIRECTIONS

Mix together butter, eggs, and sugar until creamy.

Stir in vanilla and mashed bananas.

In a separate bowl mix baking powder with flour. Mix the dry ingredients with the wet.

1 cup at a time until your batter is smooth. Pour into your spring form pan.

Pour 1 cup water into the bottom of your Instant Pot.

Place pan on a trivet and cook on manual high pressure for 50 minutes.

Do a quick release Remove and serve.

Spanish Tortilla

Total Time: 28 mins

Servings: 4

INGREDIENTS

6 large Eggs

4 oz. French Fries (defrosted)

1 Tablespoon Butter melted

1/4 cup Spanish Onions, Scallions or Onions, diced

1/2 teaspoon Sea Salt, or to taste

1/4 teaspoon Freshly Ground Black Pepper or to taste

1 teaspoon Fox Point Seasoning or other seasoning

1 clove Fresh Garlic minced

2 Tablespoons Bisquick

1/4 cup Milk

1 teaspoon Tomato Paste

4 oz. Cheese grated, any kind or a combination

1.5 cups Water

Topping

1 oz. Cheese grated

Add In Options

Green Bell Pepper

Bacon

Spinach

Ham

Sausage

DIRECTIONS

Peel and slice potatoes into thin strips and soak in water for 20 minutes.

In a medium bowl, whisk together eggs and seasonings until very frothy.

In a mixing cup, whisk together baking mix, tomato paste and milk and add to egg mixture. Whisk well. Add onions and garlic to egg mixture.

Thoroughly grease casserole dish. Remove potatoes from water and dry with a paper towel. Add raw potatoes and pour in melted butter. If using defrosted French Fries or Hash Browns, skip the melted butter.

Pour in egg mixture and any add ins and top with cheese.

Add water to Instant Pot cooking pot and place a Trivet. Place uncovered casserole dish on Trivet.

Lock on lid and close Pressure Valve. Cook on High Pressure for 15-20 minutes.

When Beep sounds, allow a 10-minute Natural Pressure Release and then release the rest of the pressure.

Top with grated cheese and place Lid on top of Instant Pot and allow cheese to melt.

Almond Milk Yogurt

Total Time: 8 hrs 15 mins

Servings: 4 cups

INGREDIENTS

4 Cups Almond Milk

1/3 Cup Raw Cashews

2 Tablespoons Arrowroot Powder

1/4 teaspoon Agar Powder

1/4 Cup Plain Almond or Coconut yogurt

1 Tablespoon Maple Syrup, optional

1 teaspoon Vanilla, Optional

DIRECTIONS

Place the first 4 ingredients into a blender and process until completely smooth. Transfer to a saucepan. Over medium heat stirring constantly bring to a simmer. Allow to simmer until the mixture has thickened about four to five minutes. Remove from heat. Transfer the mixture to a bowl (too cool) and allow cooling to 110 degrees. Stir the yogurt into the cooled mixture (and optional maple syrup and vanilla), and divide into sanitized mason jars.

While waiting for the mixture to cool sanitize the mason jars and instant pot. Add one cup of water to the instant pot liner and place the steamer rack and three clean pint jars in the liner. Place lid on Instant Pot and set knob to sealing. Steam for one minute. Remove steamer rack and discard water.

Place the filled mason jars into the instant pot liner. Place the lid on the Instant Pot and press yogurt and adjust time to 8 hours. The timer will show 8 hours and then revert back to 0, it will then count up until it reaches the time you set. Refrigerate yogurt up to two weeks.

Steamed Eggs

Total Time: 15 mins

Servings: 1-2

INGREDIENTS

Eggs

DIRECTIONS

Pour 1 cup water into the pot and position a steamer basket or trivet atop the steam rack.

Place 3-5 eggs, using canning lids or metal cookie cutters to separate/hold the eggs.

Close lid and steam valve. Press Steam setting, and adjust time down to 4 minutes. (5 minutes for hard boiled).

At end of cycle, place a cool cloth on the lid and quick release the steam valve. Use tongs to transfer eggs to cold-water for 1-2 minutes.

Blueberry Breakfast

Total Time: 6 mins

Servings: 1

INGREDIENTS

1/3 cup old fashioned oats

1/3 cup unsweetened almond milk

1/3 cup fat free Greek yogurt

1/3 cup blueberries, fresh or frozen

1 Tablespoon chia seeds

sweetener to taste

splash of vanilla

pinch of salt

sprinkle of cinnamon, optional

1-1/2 cups of water for the pot

DIRECTIONS

Pour water in your empty pot and set aside.

Using a pint size jar, pour in all ingredients in the order given.

Cover top of jar with a piece of aluminum foil and place in the pot.

Set manually for 6 minutes.

Allow your Instant Pot to release pressure naturally.

Using a pot holder or oven mitt, carefully take out jar and set it on the counter to cool for a few minutes.

Once cool enough to touch; stir oatmeal and serve.

Potatoes Casserole

Total Time: 26 mins

Servings: 6-10

INGREDIENTS

5 pounds of potatoes

1½ stick of butter

salt and pepper to taste

1 cup of milk

1 cup of sour cream

1 ranch seasoning mix

2 cups of shredded cheese

1 bundle of green onions chopped

4 slices of bacon cooked and crumbled

DIRECTIONS

Cut potatoes into chunks. Leave the skin on.

Place in the Instant pot. Add 1 cup of water, Stick butter, and salt and pepper.

Place the lid on top and make sure your nob is set to sealing.

Then click the manual button and turn it to 6 minutes.

Leave to cook until timer sounds.

Do the quick release to relieve the pressure.

Add the other butter, milk.

Mix well with an electric hand mixer right in the instant pot or mash with a hand masher.

Add in sour cream, ranch mix, and mix well.

Fold in Shredded cheese and green onions.

Place in a baking dish. Top with remaining cheese, chives, bacon.

Baked in 350-degree oven for 20 minutes.

Egg Casserole

Total Time: 35 mins

Servings: 8

INGREDIENTS

8 large eggs, well-beaten

1-pound mild ground sausage

½ large red onion, chopped

1 red bell pepper, chopped

1 can black beans, rinsed

½ cup green onions

½ cup flour

1 cup Cotija cheese

1 cup mozzarella cheese

DIRECTIONS

Turn Instant Pot on to the Sauté setting. Once it is hot, add the sausage and onion. Cook until the sausage is cooked through, about six minutes.

Mix flour with eggs until combined. Add the egg mixture to the sausage and onions in the Instant Pot.

Add chopped vegetables, beans and cheeses. You can leave a little bit of the mozzarella cheese and put that on top of the casserole when it is done.

Put the lid on the Instant Pot and lock in place.

Put the setting of the Instant Pot to the high setting and let cook for 20 minutes. When the time is up, let it depressurize and then unlock the lid.

Take the casserole out of the Instant Pot.

Breakfast Burrito Casserole

Total Time: 23 mins

Servings: 6

INGREDIENTS

4 eggs

2 pounds red potatoes- cubed

1/4 cup chopped white or yellow onion

1 diced jalapeno

6 oz. ham steak cubed

1/2 tsp salt

1/2 tsp mesquite seasoning

1/4 tsp chili powder

3/4 tsp taco seasoning-

Burrito toppings

Tortillas

DIRECTIONS

In a medium bowl mix together the salt, seasonings and eggs and 1 tablespoon water. Beat the egg gently until the yokes are broken up

Add onions, potatoes, ham and jalapeno to the bowl.

Add the mixture to the pot you plan to use inside your instant pot. If your pot has a lid use it, if not, use foil to cover the pot.

Add 1 cup of water to the bottom of your instant pot.

Add the trivet that came with your instant pot to the bottom of the pot.

On the trivet place the covered pan with the egg mixture.

Make sure the pot is set to sealing and cook on manual for 13 minutes.

Once the pot is done cooking it will beep. Let the pressure release naturally.

Carefully remove the pan from your instant pot.

Veggie Quiche

Total Time: 40 mins

Servings: 6-8

INGREDIENTS

8 large eggs

½ cup milk

½ cup flour

¼ t. salt and ¼ t. pepper

1 large red pepper, chopped

1 cup tomatoes, sliced or chopped

2 large green onions, chopped

1½ cups shredded cheese

Additional veggies

DIRECTIONS

Put trivet in the bottom of the Instant Pot.

Make an aluminum foil sling and put it in the bottom of the Instant Pot. Then add 1 cup of water.

In a large bowl, whisk eggs, milk, flour, salt and pepper. Add veggies and 1 cup of cheese until it's combined.

Pour the mixture into a bowl that will fit inside the Instant Pot bowl. Cover the bowl with aluminum foil and put the bowl on top of the trivet inside the Instant Pot.

Lock the Instant Pot lid. Select High Pressure and cook time of 30 minutes.

When timer beeps, let the Instant Pot sit and release pressure for 10 minutes.

Take the lid of the Instant Pot off, lift the bowl up using the sling and take off the aluminum foil.

Sprinkle the top of the quiche with the remaining ½ cup cheese, replace the aluminum foil and let sit until the cheese melts, about two minutes.

Peaches and Cream

Total Time: 10 mins

Servings:

4

INGREDIENTS

2 cups rolled oats

4 cups water

1 peach, chopped

1 teaspoon vanilla

Optional:

2 tablespoons flax meal

1/2 cup chopped almonds

splash of milk, cream, or non-dairy milk

maple syrup to taste

DIRECTIONS

Add oats, water, peaches, and vanilla to the Instant Pot. Set to porridge - high pressure, making sure the valve is set to sealing. Adjust the time to 3 minutes. When finished allow the pressure to release naturally for 10 minutes before doing a quick pressure release by setting the valve to venting.

Chocolate Chip Bread Pudding

Total Time: 15 mins

Servings: 1-2

INGREDIENTS

2 Cups of chopped & cubed challah bread

1 egg

¼ cup of milk

¼ cup sweetened condensed milk

½ teaspoon cinnamon

1/3 cup semi-sweet chocolate chunks

DIRECTIONS

In a medium sized bowl, add all wet ingredients and beat with a fork until well blended.

Add in your chopped challah bread and mix until all liquid is absorbed.

Add in your chocolate chunks and mix until evenly distributed.

Pour contents into your container you're going to PIP (Pot in Pot) in, such as two ramekins.

Add PIP cooking pots to the Instant Pot. Add 1 cup of water into the base of the IP pot.

Close lid and place on 11 minutes High Manual Pressure.

Once done, perform a quick release and remove lid. Allow to sit and cool.

Breakfast Cobbler

Total Time: 15 mins

Servings: 2

INGREDIENTS

1 pear, diced

1 apple, diced

1 plum, diced

2 tbsp. honey

3 tbsp. coconut oil

1/2 tsp ground cinnamon

1/4 cup unsweetened shredded coconut

1/4 cup pecan pieces

2 tbsp. sunflower seeds

DIRECTIONS

Place your cut fruit into the stainless-steel bowl of your Instant Pot.

Spoon in the honey and coconut oil, sprinkle the cinnamon, secure the lid and close off the pressure valve.

Press the Steam button; the display will read 10 minutes.

Allow the fruit to cook, and quick-release the pressure once the cooking cycle has completed.

Remove the lid once safe to do so and transfer the cooked fruit with a slotted spoon or skimmer into a serving bowl.

Now place the coconut, pecans, and sunflower seeds into the residual liquid and press the Sauté button.

Allow the contents to cook, shifting them regularly so they do not burn.

Once they are nicely browned and toasted, about 5 minutes or so, remove them and top your cooked fruit.

Breakfast Porridge

Total Time: 10 mins

Servings: 2

INGREDIENTS

1/2 cup Cashews (raw, unsalted)

1/4 cup Pepitas, shelled

1/2 cup Pecan Halves

1/2 cup Unsweetened Dried Coconut Shreds

1 cup Water

2 tsp Coconut Oil, melted

1 tbs Maple Syrup or Honey

DIRECTIONS

Combine all of the ingredients except for the water, coconut oil, and maple syrup in a blender or food processor, and blend for around 30 seconds or until the mixture becomes a meal.

Transfer the contents to the stainless-steel bowl of your Instant Pot and stir in the water, oil, and maple syrup.

Secure the lid, close off the pressure valve and press the Porridge button. Now press the "-" button until the display reads 3 minutes. Allow the porridge to cook.

Release the pressure valve and remove the lid once safe to do so. Stir the porridge once more and serve topped with fresh fruit, a bit of coconut sugar or ghee, if desired.

Red Beans and Rice

Total Time: 10 mins

Servings: 8

INGREDIENTS

1 medium onion diced

1 bell pepper diced

3 celery stalks diced

3 cloves garlic minced

1 pound of dry red kidney beans

1 tsp salt or more to taste

1/2 tsp black pepper

1/4 tsp white pepper (optional)

1 tsp hot sauce (I used Texas Pete.)

1 tsp fresh thyme or ½ tsp dried thyme

2 leaves bay

7 cups water

1 pound of chicken andouille sausage cut into thin slices

10 cups cooked rice

DIRECTIONS

Add all ingredients, except for sausage and rice to the Instant Pot.

Place the lid on, lock it, and set to manual high pressure for 28 minutes.

At the end of the 28 minutes, use the quick release method (release the valve).

When the Instant Pot is fully depressurized the pin will fall, and you can remove the lid.

Run the lid under cold water, and set aside. This will help the Instant Pot to re-seal.

Add the chicken andouille sausage, place the lid on and lock it.

Use the manual setting at 15 minutes high pressure, and allow the Instant Pot to release naturally this time.

You can let the beans mixture sit with the lid off for a few minutes to thicken the liquid.

Serve the bean mixture over a cup of cooked rice.

Teriyaki Turkey Meatballs

Total Time: 15 mins

Servings: 4

INGREDIENTS

1 lb ground turkey meat

5 saltine crackers, crushed

3 tablespoons buttermilk

¼ cup green onion, sliced + more for garnish

1 teaspoon garlic powder

1/2 teaspoon kosher salt

Black pepper to taste

1 tablespoons canola oil

1 tablespoon sesame seeds

Teriyaki Sauce:

1/2 cup low sodium soy sauce

1/4 cup rice vinegar

2 cloves garlic, minced

2 teaspoons fresh grated ginger

2 tablespoons canola oil

3 tablespoons brown sugar

1/4 teaspoon black pepper

1 tablespoon corn starch

Get Ingredients Powered by Chicory

DIRECTIONS

In a large bowl combine ground turkey, crushed crackers, buttermilk, green onions, salt and pepper. Gently shape into 16 meatballs.

Combine teriyaki sauce ingredients in a medium bowl. Set aside.

Heat the Instant Pot in sauté mode. Add 1 tablespoon of oil and brown the meatballs, about 2 minutes per side. When brown add the teriyaki sauce, cover and lock the lid. Cook high pressure 10 minutes.

After 10 minutes, turn off the pot and allow it to release pressure naturally. This will take about 5 minutes.

Sprinkle with sliced green onions and sesame seeds. Serve with rice or quinoa.

Beef Gyros

Total Time: 15 mins

Servings: 4

INGREDIENTS

2 lbs beef roast thinly sliced

3 cloves minced garlic

1 tbsp dried parsley

1 tsp black pepper

1 tsp salt

1/2 cup vegetable broth

1 red onion thinly sliced

1 tbsp lemon juice

4 tbsp oil

1 tsp apple cider vinegar (optional)

1 tsp olive oil (optional)

Toppings

Pitas or Naan bread

Sliced carrots

Sliced onions

Sliced cucumbers

Lettuce

Feta or goat cheese (optional, use container to measure)

Tzatziki Sauce:

1 cup plain Greek yogurt

1/2 cup cucumber peeled seeded, and chopped

1 clove minced garlic

1 tsp salt and pepper

2 tbsp fresh dill

DIRECTIONS

Turn Instant Pot on sauté and let the pan warn up. When it's warm, add oil to the bottom of the pan and let it get hot.

Add meat, seasoning, garlic, and onion to Instant Pot. Sear and let onions soften for 3-5 minutes

Pour lemon juice and broth over the meat. Give the meat a quick stir, then lock lid into place. Turn the steam valve to sealing. Using the Meat/Stew preset cook the gyro meat for 9 minutes. Let the pressure naturally release for 3 minutes before releasing the remaining pressure using the quick release method.

While the gyro meat is cooking mix together the Tzatziki sauce and slice your vegetable toppings. For added flavor drizzle apple cider vinegar and olive oil over vegetables.

To make your gyro layer the lettuce at the bottom of the pita or naan bread. Then add your meat, toppings, and sauce. This will keep the pita or naan from getting soggy.

Paleo Beef Barbacoa

Total Time: 1 hr. 5 mins

Servings: 1-2

INGREDIENTS

3 pounds grass-fed chuck roast, fat cut off and cut into large chunks

1 large onion, peeled and sliced

6 garlic cloves

2- 4oz cans of green chilis

1 tablespoon oregano

1 teaspoon salt

1 teaspoons pepper

3 dried chipotle peppers, stems removed and broken into pieces

juice of 3 limes

3 tablespoons coconut vinegar

1 tablespoon cumin

1/2 cup water

DIRECTIONS

Add all ingredients to the Instant Pot and stir.

Place lid on, make sure vent is closed, and hit the "manual" button. Increase time to 60 minutes.

Once done, let naturally release or press "cancel" and release the pressure.

Remove lid, shred with a fork, and hit the "sauté" button. Stir regularly as the juices reduce. This may take up to 30 minutes to fully reduce.

Buffalo Chicken Meatballs

Total Time: 1 hr 5 mins

Servings: 18-24 meatballs

INGREDIENTS

1.5 lb ground chicken

¾ cup almond meal

1 tsp sea salt

2 garlic cloves, minced

2 green onions, thinly sliced

2 tbsp ghee

6 tbsp hot sauce

4 tbsp butter or ghee

chopped green onions, for garnish

DIRECTIONS

In a large bowl, combine chicken, almond meal, salt, minced garlic cloves, and green onions.

Use your hands to combine everything together, but be careful not to overwork the meat.

Grease your hands with ghee or coconut oil, then shape the meat into balls 1-2 inches wide.

Set your Instant Pot to sauté setting and add ghee.

Working in batches, gently place the chicken meatballs in the Instant Pot to brown them. Turn them every minute until all sides are brown.

While the meatballs are browning, combine hot sauce and butter or ghee and heat them in the microwave or the stove top until the butter is completely melted. Use a spoon to stir. This is your buffalo sauce.

Place all the browned meatballs in the Instant Pot, and then pour the buffalo sauce evenly over the meatballs.

Screw on the lid to the Instant Pot, make sure that the pressure valve is set to "sealing," then set it to "Poultry."

Once the meatballs are finished cooking (about 15-20 minutes), the Instant Pot will beep. If you are eating right away, hit "Cancel" then release the pressure valve, making sure your hand is away from the opening where the steam escapes. If not, the Instant Pot will automatically switch to the "Warm" setting for the next 10 hours and the pressure will slowly lower on its own.

Serve over rice, cauliflower rice, zoodles. Or just eat on its own!

Shepherd's Pie

Total Time: 30 mins

Servings: 6-8

INGREDIENTS

4 russet baking potatoes, peeled and cut into 1" cubes

salt, divided

1 egg

1 tsp garlic powder

2 Tbsp butter

1 lb ground beef

1 onion, diced

3 carrots, peeled & cut into 1/2" pieces

1 C chopped mushrooms

1 C frozen peas

1 C beef broth

3 Tbsp flour

1 C cheddar cheese

DIRECTIONS

Combine potatoes, 1 cup water, and 1 teaspoon salt in the Instant Pot. Cook on high pressure for 8 minutes. Drain the potatoes and transfer to a mixing bowl. Add 1 egg, 1 teaspoon salt, 1 teaspoon garlic powder, and 2 tablespoons butter to the potatoes. Mash the potato mixture with a masher, or whip with a hand mixer.

In the now-empty Instant Pot, sauté the ground beef for 5 minutes until it begins to brown. Add the carrots, onions, peas, mushrooms, and 1 tsp each salt and pepper. Stir to combine. Mix together beef broth and flour in a small measuring cup, then pour the broth mixture into the Instant Pot and stir to combine again. Top the beef mixture with the mashed potatoes and smooth the top of the potatoes with a spatula. Cook on high pressure for 10 minutes.

Quick release the pressure. Immediately top with shredded cheese and serve.

Beef Stroganoff

Total Time: 27 mins

Servings: 6-8

INGREDIENTS

2 Tbsp EVOO

1/2 onion, diced

1 piece of bacon, chopped into 1/4" pieces

2 tsp salt, divided

1 tsp freshly ground pepper

1 lb sirloin roast, cut into 1" pieces

3 garlic cloves, minced

1/2 tsp dried thyme

3 C chopped mushrooms

2 Tbsp flour

1 C beef broth

2 C chicken broth

8oz wide egg noodles

1/2 C heavy cream

2 C chopped spinach

DIRECTIONS

Turn IP on Sauté and add 2 Tbsp olive oil to the bottom of the pot. Give the oil a minute to heat up, then add the diced onions, bacon, and 1/2 tsp salt to the pot. Sauté for 3-4 minutes, until the bacon starts to brown and the onion begins to soften.

Season the roast pieces with 1 tsp salt and the freshly ground pepper. Add the meat to the onion and bacon and stir to combine. Brown the meat for about 2 minutes, stirring a couple of times to sear it evenly on all sides. Add the minced garlic and the thyme to the pot, cook for 30 seconds or until the garlic is fragrant.

Add the chopped mushrooms to the pot, and then the flour. Stir the flour into the mixture to coat the ingredients. Immediately pour in both broths and 1/2 tsp of salt. Add the egg noodles and stir well to evenly distribute the ingredients. Cover the IP, close the pressure valve, and cook on high pressure for 17 minutes.

After 17 minutes on high pressure, quick release the pressure and switch back to Sauté. Pour in the cream and stir to combine. Continue to cook the stroganoff for about 5 more minutes to let the sauce thicken.

Remove the pot from the heat and stir in the spinach. Add additional seasoning as desired. Serve immediately.

Mac n' Cheese

Total Time: 44 mins

Servings: 6-8

INGREDIENTS

3 bacon slices, chopped

2 garlic cloves, minced

3 1/2 C water

4 C dried pasta

2 Tbsp flour

1 1/2 C milk

4oz cream cheese

2 C shredded cheddar cheese

2 C frozen peas, thawed

DIRECTIONS

Heat the Instant Pot on the sauté function. Add the chopped bacon, and cook for 2 to 3 minutes until the bacon begins to crisp. Stir in the minced garlic and sauté for about 30 more seconds. Pour in 3 1/2 cups of water, and stir in the dried pasta. Cover the Instant Pot and cook on high pressure for 5 minutes.

Let the pressure naturally release for 5 minutes, then quick release the remaining pressure.

Combine the flour and milk and whisk until smooth. Pour the milk mixture into the Instant Pot. Turn the IP back onto sauté, and simmer the pasta until the milk begins to thicken, about 4-5 minutes. Cut the cream cheese into 1" pieces and stir it into the pasta until it melts and is completely mixed in. Stir in the cheddar cheese until melted.

Add the peas to the mac'n'cheese. Serve when warm. Salt to taste.

Asian Ramen Noodles

Total Time: 10 mins

Servings: 1-2

INGREDIENTS

2 tsp sesame oil

1 chicken breast, butterflied & cut into thin strips

1 carrot, peeled and sliced in thin strips

1/2 onion, sliced thin

1/2 C broccoli, sliced in thin pieces

1 tsp granulated garlic

1 tsp ginger powder

2 pieces dried ramen noodles

1 C water

2 Tbsp low sodium soy sauce

1/2 C peanuts (optional)

DIRECTIONS

Turn the Instant Pot onto Sauté. Add 2 tsp sesame oil to the bottom of the pot, then add the chicken, carrots, onions, and broccoli. Add the garlic and ginger, stir to coat, and sauté for 3 minutes, turning the ingredients so that the chicken is completely browned.

Transfer the chicken mixture to a bowl so that the Instant Pot is empty. Pour the water and soy sauce into the pot, set the ramen noodles in the water, and then return the chicken mixture to the IP. Place the lid on the IP, close the pressure valve, and set it to cook on high pressure for 1 minute.

After 1 minute on high pressure, quick release the pressure. Stir the noodles and serve immediately. Add peanuts and additional soy sauce as desired.

Delicious Chili

Total Time: 30 mins

Servings: 8

Ingredients:

1 tbsp vegetable oil

2 tsp minced garlic

1 lb lean ground beef

1 large onion, chopped

1 large bell pepper, chopped

6 stalks celery, chopped

1 package McCormick's Chili Seasoning

1 cup water

1 15 oz can Ranch Style Beans

1 15 oz can dark red kidney beans, drained

1 15 oz can RoTel Original

1 15 oz can diced tomatoes

1 15 oz can tomato sauce

Salt and pepper to taste

DIRECTIONS

Set your Instant Pot to Sauté and vegetable oil and minced garlic to the pot.

Once the pot is hot and oil is simmering, add ground beef.

Once browned, add chopped onion, bell pepper and celery to the beef.

Cook until onion is starting to become translucent, then add McCormick's Chili Seasoning.

Mix well and add water.

Scrape up any browned bits that have adhered to the bottom of the pot.

Add Ranch Style and kidney beans to the pot and stir.

Then add Rotel, diced tomatoes and tomato sauce on top.

Then add your Instant Pot lid, make sure vent is set to seal and set your IP to 10 minutes on manual.

Once time is up, let your Instant Pot naturally release.

Once released, open your Instant Pot, stir and enjoy your chili!

Pulled Chicken

Total Time: 37 mins

Servings: 10

INGREDIENTS

2 tablespoons vegetable oil

1 large onion sliced

2 to 3 cloves garlic chopped

5 pounds chicken breast

3 cups of salsa

DIRECTIONS

Uses the sauté function of the Instant Pot. When the oil is hot add the onions. Sauté until almost translucent, then add the garlic.

Add chicken breast and salsa.

Cook on high on the manual setting for 20 minutes.

Perform a quick release on the Instant Pot. Remove chicken and shred.

Some people love to shred chicken in the stand mixers, by using the mixer blades on low speed.

Chipotle Barbacoa

Total Time: 55 mins

Servings: 1-2

INGREDIENTS

6 to 8 pounds boneless chuck roast, trimmed of excess fat and cut into 2 inch cubes

1 tablespoon vegetable oil or canola oil

6 chipotles in adobo with sauce

1 large white onion, peeled and roughly chopped

10 cloves garlic, peeled and roughly chopped

1 cup beef broth

2/3 cup apple cider vinegar (I use bragg's)

½ cup lime juice

2 tablespoons cumin

2 tablespoons dried oregano

1 tablespoon chili powder

1 tablespoon celtic sea salt

½ teaspoon ground cloves

DIRECTIONS

In a large blender, add adobo, onion, garlic, vinegar, lime juice, cumin, oregano, chili powder, salt, and cloves.

Blend until smooth.

Set aside.

In an instant pot, heat oil on high sauté, and brown meat in small batches.

When meat is browned, add sauce from blender.

Add stock, set valve to seal, and cook on high pressure for 50 minutes.

Force release, shred, and add to burritos!

Apple Cider Pork Loin

Total Time: 1 hr 15 mins

Servings: 1

INGREDIENTS

2 tablespoons vegetable oil

1 large sliced white onion

1/4 teaspoon salt

2 tablespoons garlic

salt and pepper to season roast

5 to 6-pound pork loin

1 1/2 cups hard cider

DIRECTIONS

If you are using hard cider, measure out your hard cider, and allow it to go flat while you prepare the remaining part of the recipe.

Set the Instant Pot to sauté.

Add 2 tablespoons of vegetable oil to the pot.

Heat oil until it is hot.

Add sliced onion, garlic, and a pinch of salt.

Sauté until the onions are almost translucent.

Sauté roast on all sides until it just begins to brown.

Add flat hard cider; place the lid on the Instant Pot.

Pressure cook for 55 minutes on the manual setting.

Once the roast has finished cooking you can perform a quick release.

Delicious Chicken

Total Time: 35 mins

Servings: 1-2

INGREDIENTS

6-8 slices cooked bacon

2 pounds boneless chicken breast

1 packet ranch seasoning

8oz cream cheese

1 cup water

3 tbs corn starch

4oz cheddar cheese

DIRECTIONS

Place chicken and cream cheese in the IP.

Sprinkle the packet of ranch seasoning over the top.

Add one cup water.

Place your IP on Manual high pressure for 25 minutes.

Do a quick release.

Remove chicken only and shred I used my kitchen aid to shred my chicken.

Keep your IP on low and Mix in cornstarch with a whisk.

Add cheese and shredded chicken to the mixture.

Stir in bacon and enjoy.

Ranch Pot Roast

Total Time: 50 mins

Servings: 6

INGREDIENTS

2 tbsp sunflower coconut oil

4-5 lb pot roast

3 large carrots, peeled and sliced into rounds

4 stalks celery, sliced thin

2 cups chicken stock

1 ranch dressing packet

1 tsp celtic sea salt

1 tsp pepper

DIRECTIONS

Turn instant pot to sauté setting.

Add oil, heat until shimmery.

Add pot roast, let brown on each side (about 6 minutes per side).

Remove pot roast, set aside.

Add celery, carrots to pan.

Cook until soft and lightly browned, about 5 minutes on sauté.

Deglaze with stock. Add roast back into pan.

Add ranch dressing packet to season.

Add lid to instant pot, set to seal.

Cook on meat with high pressure for 38 minutes, and let naturally release.

Remove pot roast from pan.

Set instant pot to sauté and reduce sauce to thick gravy.

Pour gravy over roast and serve immediately.

Zuppa Toscana

Total Time: 15 mins

Servings: 1-2

INGREDIENTS

2 Tbs olive oil

1 medium onion, diced

1 lb ground mild Italian sausage

4 cloves garlic, minced

3 large russet potatoes unpeeled and sliced into 1/4-inch slices.

6 cups (1 1/2 quarts) chicken broth

1/4 cup water

2 cups fresh kale, chiffonade

3/4 cup heavy cream or half and half

DIRECTIONS

Using the "sauté" function of the Instant Pot, heat the olive oil. Add onions and cook until they begin to become translucent.

Add the Italian sausage, crumbling up into smaller pieces and cooking until browned.

Add garlic and allow cooking just until fragrant, about a minute.

Drain off excess grease if desired and return to pot.

Add potato slices, chicken broth and water.

Lock the lid into place and set to "sealed."

Cook at high pressure for 5 minutes using the Manual setting.

When cooking is complete, allow a natural pressure release for 10 minutes, followed by a quick release.

When pressure valve has dropped, remove the lid and add kale to the pot. The heat from the soup will wilt the kale as you stir.

Pour in cream or half and half (or milk), stirring to combine.

Chicken Enchiladas

Total Time: 40 mins

Servings: 12

INGREDIENTS

2 Tbs olive oil

1 medium onion, diced

1 lb ground mild Italian sausage

4 cloves garlic, minced

3 large russet potatoes unpeeled and sliced into 1/4-inch slices.

6 cups (1 1/2 quarts) chicken broth

1/4 cup water

2 cups fresh kale, chiffonade

3/4 cup heavy cream or half and half

DIRECTIONS

Using the "sauté" function of the Instant Pot, heat the olive oil. Add onions and cook until they begin to become translucent.

Add the Italian sausage, crumbling up into smaller pieces and cooking until browned.

Add garlic and allow cooking just until fragrant, about a minute.

Drain off excess grease if desired and return to pot.

Add potato slices, chicken broth and water.

Lock the lid into place and set to "sealed."

Cook at high pressure for 5 minutes using the Manual setting.

When cooking is complete, allow a natural pressure release for 10 minutes, followed by a quick release.

When pressure valve has dropped, remove the lid and add kale to the pot. The heat from the soup will wilt the kale as you stir.

Pour in cream or half and half (or milk), stirring to combine.

Swedish Meatballs

Total Time: 15 mins

Servings: 1-2

INGREDIENTS

1.5 cups low sodium beef broth

1 cup milk

(2) 12 oz boxes cream of mushroom soup (mixed with only 1 box of water for both)

16 oz egg noodles

(1) 24oz bag fully cooked frozen meatballs

1 cup sour cream

DIRECTIONS

First, add beef broth, milk, cream of mushroom soup and water into the Instant Pot.

Next, add in the package of egg noodles into the Instant Pot.

Layer the meatballs on top of the egg noodles in a single layer.

Manually set the Instant Pot to cook for 12 minutes, sealed.

When there's 2 minutes of cook time remaining, carefully (using a kitchen hand towel - the steam is super hot!) release the steam valve to venting.

Once the steam has completely released, carefully open the lid of instant pot away from you.

Stir in one cup of sour cream and mix thoroughly.

Serve & enjoy!

Steak Tacos

Total Time: 10 mins

Servings: 6

INGREDIENTS

8 oz sirloin steak fat trimmed and sliced into thin pieces

1/2 cup red onion chopped

1/4 cup tomatoes chopped

3/4 cup reduced-fat Mexican cheese shredded

2 tbsp crema or sour cream

6 tbsp authentic salsa one tablespoon per taco

1 tbsp olive oil

2 tbsp cilantro chopped

Trader Joe's Taco Seasoning to taste

McCormick's Grill Mates Steak Rub and pepper to taste

DIRECTIONS

Turn the Instant Pot on the sauté' function. When the pot displays "Hot" add the olive oil to the pot.

Season the steak with the seasonings. Add the steak to the pot.

Cook both sides of the steak for 2-3 minutes until the steak turns brown.

Remove the steak from the pot. Top the steak with cheese immediately if you prefer melted cheese on your tacos.

Turn the oven on Broil. When heated, add the corn tortillas to the oven. Place the tortillas directly on an oven rack. Allow the tortillas to warm for a couple of minutes.

Remove the tortillas and add the steak, crema, salsa, and tomatoes. Sprinkle the cilantro throughout.

Baby Carrots with Mint

Total Time: 15 mins

Servings: 4

INGREDIENTS

1 pound (16 ounces) package Baby Carrots

1 cup Water

1 tablespoon Unsalted Butter

1 tablespoon chopped fresh Mint Leaves (plus extra as garnish if desired)

Sea Salt

6 qt Instant Pot

DIRECTIONS

Combine the carrots and water in the Instant Pot insert. Seal the lid, set the pressure vent on SEALING and select MANUAL, HIGH PRESSURE for 2 minutes.

When the time is complete, QUICK RELEASE the pressure, and pour the carrots into a strainer to drain. Wipe out the insert, return it to the Instant Pot and select SAUTÉ. Add the butter and stir while it melts. Add the mint and sauté for about 30 seconds to release the flavor and aroma of the mint.

Add the carrots back into the insert, sauté to coat, remove, sprinkle lightly with sea salt and serve immediately.

Chicken Fettuccini Alfredo

Total Time: 20 mins

Servings: 4

INGREDIENTS

1 tbsp olive oil

1/2 tsp kosher salt

1/4 tsp black pepper

2 chicken breasts, boneless and skinless

2 tbsp salted butter

5 cloves garlic, minced

2 C heavy cream

2 C chicken broth

1/4 tsp kosher salt

1 pinch of ground nutmeg

1 lb dry fettuccini noodles

1/2 C parmesan cheese, shredded

fresh basil

DIRECTIONS

Press sauté button on Instant Pot and heat olive oil until display reads "HOT". Season chicken breasts with salt and pepper and place in the pot to brown. Cook 2 minutes per side just until lightly browned, but not cooked all the way through, remove from pot and place on a plate.

Melt butter in the pot and stir in minced garlic. Cook for less than 1 minute, stirring constantly until fragrant and pour in cream.

Bring cream and garlic to a simmer while scraping the bottom of the pot with a spatula to release the browned bits from cooking the chicken. Simmer sauce for 2 minutes until just slightly thickened and pour in chicken broth, salt and nutmeg.

Break dry noodles in half and place into the pot, followed by the browned chicken breasts.

Cover Instant Pot and set it to cook at High Pressure for 6 minutes.

When time is up, allow Instant Pot to naturally release pressure-- about 8 minutes (See Notes).

Remove chicken and slice if desired before returning to the pot. Stir in cheese and fresh chopped basil before serving.

PIZZA PASTA

Total Time: 15 mins

Servings: 6

INGREDIENTS

1 lb. sausage, Italian, mild,

8 oz. pizza sauce

16 oz. pasta sauce

28 oz. water

8 oz. mozzarella

20 slices pizza pepperoni

1 lb. pasta (I used cavatappi)

2 tsp garlic, minced

1 tsp Italian seasoning

as desired salt and pepper

1 tbsp. butter

DIRECTIONS

Set the IP on "sauté". Melt the butter; add the garlic Italian seasoning and sausage. Sauté until the sausage is no longer pink.

Add both spaghetti sauce and pizza sauce to the sausage mixture. Next add in pasta.

Add the water. Give a stir and put on the lid, and be sure to set the toggle switch to "seal"

Set on Manual for 5 minutes. Do a Quick Release and open the lid after the silver pin has dropped.

Add HALF the cheese and HALF the pepperoni – mix it into the pasta/meat mixture

Sprinkle the remaining cheese and pepperoni over the top of the mixture. Replace the lid and let the cheese melt and the pepperoni warm through.

Ricotta

Total Time: 35 mins

Servings: 6

INGREDIENTS

4 cups whole milk

2 tbs white vinegar

DIRECTIONS

Pour the milk into the Instant Pot, close the lid, and set the vent to Sealing.

Press the Yogurt button and press Adjust until you see Boil.

Let the pot run the boil cycle. When it beeps, it means the milk has reached 180 degrees. Release the pressure and remove the top.

Remove the inner pot to a trivet and pour the vinegar into the milk. Stir briefly. You'll see the ricotta separating from the liquid. Let the mixture sit for 10 minutes.

Transfer the ricotta mixture to a fine mesh strainer lined with butter muslin. Let the liquid drain for a couple minutes, and add a sprinkle of salt if desired. Transfer the mixture to an airtight container and refrigerate.

Pumpkin Chocolate Bundt Cake

Total Time: 57 mins

Servings: 12

INGREDIENTS

3/4 cup whole wheat flour

3/4 cup unbleached all-purpose flour

1/2 teaspoon salt

1 teaspoon baking soda

1/2 teaspoon baking powder

3/4 teaspoon pumpkin pie spice

3/4 cup sugar

1 medium banana mashed

2 Tablespoons canola oil

1/2 cup 2% Greek yogurt

1/2 15 ounce can 100% pureed pumpkin

1 egg

1/2 teaspoon pure vanilla extract

2/3 cup semi sweet chocolate chips or chocolate chunks

DIRECTIONS

In a medium bowl, combine flour, salt, baking soda, baking powder, pumpkin pie spice; set aside.

Use an electric mixer to combine the sugar, banana, oil, yogurt, pureed pumpkin, egg and vanilla (separate bowl from dry ingredients).

With the mixer on low, gradually add the dry ingredients until incorporated.

Fold in the chocolate chips.

Grease the bundt pan (or use cooking spray), and transfer the batter to the bundt pan.

Cover the pan with paper towels and then foil.

Add 1.5 cups water to the inner stainless steel pot in the Instant Pot, and place the trivet inside.

Place the bundt pan on top, place the lid on and lock it.

Use the manual button, and set it to 35 minutes.

Let the pressure release naturally for 10 minutes, then release the valve and remove the lid.

Let the pan cool for a few minutes before trying to remove it.

Mini Lava Cake

Total Time: 15 mins

Servings: 3

INGREDIENTS

Egg

2 Tbsp Extra Virgin Olive Oil

4 Tbsp Sugar

4 Tbsp Milk (we used Raw)

4 Tbsp All Purpose, Organic Unbleached Flour

1 Tbsp Cacao Powder

Pinch of Salt

1/2 tsp Baking Powder

DIRECTIONS

Grease your ramekins with a little butter or oil and set aside.

In your Instant Pot, pour 1 C. of water, and place the trivet inside the inner pot.

In a medium bowl, mix up all of the ingredients listed above until well blended.

Pour into your ramekins - and fill just shy of the top of each.

Place the ramekins inside the Instant Pot, put the lid on top, and close the valve.

Set the Instant Pot to 6 minutes, or 9 minutes for more of a cake-like result.

Once the pot beeps, remove the ramekins and sprinkle the tops with powdered sugar, if desired.

Red Velvet Lava Cake

Total Time: 50 mins

Servings: 3

INGREDIENTS

Box of Red Velvet Cake Mix

3 eggs

oil

water

Plus you need

1/4 cup of sugar

8oz cream cheese

DIRECTIONS

First, you will take the cream cheese out of the fridge for at least 30 minutes to get to room temp.

Once you feel the cream cheese is at room temp and soft.

You will mix the sugar and cream cheese together in a bowl.

Roll your cream cheese into 3 inch balls then place in the fridge.

You will now get out the cake mix box and mix up the cake mix together.

Now get out 3 small Pyrex dishes (1 cup size glass dishes).

Spray them with cooking spray.

Now take your cream cheese balls out of the fridge and set next to your mix and glass dishes.

Now simply fill each glass a little under 1/2 full.

Now place your cream cheese balls and then fill up the glass dish to almost full.

Last you will place on your trivet on the bottom of your Instant Pot with one cup of water.

Place the lid on your Instant Pot; close the lid place on manual mode for 14 minutes.

Once the timer goes off, do a manual release open the lid and grab your trivet to lift them out.

You should be able to grab your glass dishes with a dish rag or pot holder and flip them out so you can enjoy warm.

Chocolate Cheesecake

Total Time: 45 mins

Servings: 1

INGREDIENTS

Crust:

5 Tbsp unsalted butter, melted and then cooled

2 C. chocolate cookie or graham cracker crumbs

Cheesecake:

8 oz dark chocolate

1 lb cream cheese, room temperature

1/4 C. brown sugar

1/4 C. granulated sugar

2 egg yolks, room temperature

1 whole egg, room temperature

1/4 C. sour cream, regular, room temperature

1 tsp vanilla extract

1/4 C. cocoa powder

Ganache:

1 C. heavy cream

8 oz semi-sweet chocolate

DIRECTIONS

Prepare your Instant Pot by adding 2 C. of water in the pressure cooker and then placing the trivet inside.

Pull out two long pieces of tin foil (2 feet long) and fold them lengthwise to make a sling that is 4 layers thick. Set that aside.

Chop up your 8 oz of chocolate and melt it in a stainless-steel bowl over warm water - do not let the water touch the chocolate.

Combine the melted butter with the chocolate crumbs and make a crust for your cheesecake - pour the crumbs in the springform pan and push them down to make a nice, even layer - you'll want to push those crumbs up the side of the springform just a bit, then put the springform pan in the freezer for a little while, as you make the cheesecake filling.

In your KitchenAid, cream the room temperature cream cheese with the sugars, adding in the eggs one at a time until well blended. Once the eggs are all in, add the melted chocolate, sour cream and vanilla, and beat on high, scrape down the sides of the bowl as needed.

Blend the filling until creamy.

Pour the filling into the springform pan atop the crust, and smooth the top down evenly with a spatula.

Place the pan on the sling and carefully move to your Instant Pot. Lower the pan into the Instant Pot (sling being on the underside), then fold the ends down so as to avoid them touching the top of the cheesecake.

Place the lid on the Instant Pot, close the valve, and set the pot for manual (high) for 25 minutes.

Once the pot beeps, do a quick release and the cheesecake should be puffy - that is NORMAL.

Gently and carefully untuck the ends of the sling out and lift the cheesecake out, setting it on your counter to cool for the next hour.

Once cooled on the counter for an hour, transfer the cheesecake to the fridge and let it chill before serving - preferably 4-5 hours if not overnight.

Once cooled, make the ganache. Cut the chocolate in pieces and combine with heavy cream on low heat. Stir frequently to avoid the mixture from sticking or burning to the pan. Once blended, remove from heat and let cool slightly before adding to the top of the cheesecake. Keep refrigerated.

Orange Marmalade

Total Time: 35 mins

Servings: 6 jars

INGREDIENTS

2 1/2 pounds of fresh oranges

1 Meyer lemon (large)

1 cup of water

7 cups sugar to taste

Candy Thermometer

DIRECTIONS

First, wash the oranges and lemon.

Next, slice the oranges and lemons thin with a mandolin. Add one up of water with all juices.

The last thing you do is close your lid and turn your Instant Pot on to manual for 10 minutes and cook on high.

After the timer goes off you will let it natural release the pressure for 10-15 minutes.

Now open the lid in and turn sauté and slow add in the sugar stirring and using a candy thermometer get the temp to 212.

Once the temperature reaches 212, turn off the Instant Pot and still stir for a few minutes while the temperature drops down.

Wash oranges well, slice thin using a mandolin, quarter the slices, do the same with the lemon, add all including the juice to the instant pot, add one cup of water, and manual 10 minutes NPR.

Apple Crisp

Total Time: 13 mins

Servings: 1-2

INGREDIENTS

5 medium sized apples, peeled and chopped into chunks

2 tsp cinnamon

1/2 tsp nutmeg

1/2 cup water

1 tbsp maple syrup

4 tbsp butter

3/4 cup old fashioned rolled oats

1/4 cup flour

1/4 cup brown sugar

1/2 tsp salt

DIRECTIONS

Place apples on the bottom of your Instant Pot. Sprinkle with cinnamon and nutmeg. Top with water and maple syrup.

Melt the butter. In a small bowl, mix together melted butter, oats, flour, brown sugar and salt. Drop by the spoonful on top of the apples.

Secure the lid on the instant pot. Use the manual setting, and cook on high pressure for 8 minutes.

Use a natural release. Let sit for a few minutes, the sauce will thicken.

Serve warm and maybe top with vanilla ice cream.

Salted Caramel Cheesecake

Total Time: 4 hrs 40 mins

Servings: 1-2

INGREDIENTS

Crust

1½ cups finely crushed ritz, about 1½ sleeves

4 tablespoons butter, melted

2 tablespoons sugar

Cheesecake

16 ounces cream cheese, room temperature

½ cup light brown sugar

¼ cup sour cream

1 tablespoon flour

½ teaspoon kosher salt

1½ teaspoons vanilla

2 eggs

Topping

½ cup caramel sauce

1 teaspoon flaked sea salt

DIRECTIONS

Spray a 7- inch Springform pan lightly with cooking spray. Cut a piece of parchment paper to fit the bottom of the pan and spray again. Set aside.

In a large bowl combine the Ritz crumbs, butter and sugar evenly. Press the mixture firmly into the bottom and up the sides of the prepared pan. Set aside.

In the bowl of your stand mixer beat the cream cheese and sugar until combined and even. Add in the sour cream and mix for 30 more seconds until smooth, add in the flour, salt and vanilla, scraping the sides of the bowl as necessary. Finally add in the eggs and mix until just smooth. Don't over-mix.

Pour the cream cheese mixture into the prepared crust.

Pour 2 cups of water into the bottom of your Instant Pot. place the trivet that came with the pot into the bottom. Cut a piece of aluminum foil the same size as a paper towel. Place the foil under the paper towel and put the springform pan on top of the paper towel. Wrap the bottom of the pan in the foil, with the paper towel as a barrier.

Next take another piece of foil about 18- inches long folded into thirds long-wise. Place this under the Springform pan and use the two sides as a "sling" to place the cheesecake into the pot. It will also make it very easy to remove the cheesecake from the Instant Pot when it's done.

Once the pan is in the Instant Pot secure the lid and press the manual button. Adjust the pressure to high and set for 35 minutes, making sure the vent is closed.

Let the cheesecake cook and then allow the pressure to release naturally.

Remove the cheesecake from the pot using the sling you prepared and place on a wire rack to cool the cheesecake for an hour. Cover the cheesecake in the pan with foil and place int he refrigerator to chill for at least 4 hours or overnight.

When you're ready to serve, top the cheesecake with the caramel sauce and sprinkle with sea salt. Using a butter knife loosen the sides of the cheesecake from the pan and release the sides of the pan.

Store airtight refrigerated for up to 5 days.

Applesauce

Total Time: 15 mins

Servings: 1-2

INGREDIENTS

6-8 medium to large apples

1 cup water

1-2 drops cinnamon essential oil

1 tsp organic cinnamon

DIRECTIONS

Cut apples into 2-inch chunks. Discard the core, stem and seeds.

Place in Instant Pot along with 1 cup of water.

Close Instant Pot lid and set to manual high pressure (HP) for 8 minutes. Be sure the steam vent is sealed.

The Instant Pot will take about 8 minutes to reach high pressure, and then will cook for 8 minutes.

Once the timer goes off, let sit for about 2-3 minutes.

Turn steam vent to release pressure. Once all steam has dissipated, open the lid.

Remove excess water if there is any.

Use an electric mixer or immersion blender to smooth out applesauce to the consistency you prefer. I like mine with some lumpiness to it. You may prefer it smooth.

Add 1-2 drops of cinnamon oil or cinnamon powder to taste.

Let cool or place in the refrigerator to cool down.

Mini-Lemon Cheesecakes

Total Time: 18 mins

Servings: 6

INGREDIENTS

6 half pint mason jars

16 oz cream cheese, room temp

½ cup sugar

1 tsp flour

½ tsp vanilla

¼ cup sour cream, room temp

1 TBSP Lemon Juice

zest of one lemon

3 eggs, room temp

1 jar lemon curd

raspberries

1.5 cups water

DIRECTIONS

In a large mixing bowl, beat together cream cheese, sugar, and flour until mixture is creamy with no lumps.

Beat in vanilla, sour cream, lemon juice, and lemon zest just until mixed well. Beat in one egg at a time just until mixed. Do not overbeat.

Fill each jar with ¼ cup of cheesecake batter. Gently drop 1TBSP of lemon curd on top of batter. Add an additional ¼ cup cheesecake batter to each jar on top of the lemon curd. Loosely cover each jar with foil.

Add 1.5 cups of water to the bottom of the Instant Pot. Place the trivet on the bottom. Arrange three jars on top of the trivet. Stack the other three jars on the first three. Secure the lid to the Instant Pot, making sure the vent is in the pressure cooking position.

Manually cook on high pressure for 8 minutes. Do a natural pressure release for at least 15 minutes. With a hot pad or towel, carefully remove the jars from the Instant Pot. Cool to room temperature and store in the refrigerator until ready to serve.

Garnish with additional lemon curd and raspberries.

Oreo Cheesecake

Total Time: 55 mins

Servings: 6

INGREDIENTS

For the Crust

12 whole Oreo cookies, crushed into crumbs

2 tablespoons salted butter, melted

For the Cheesecake

16 ounces cream cheese, room temperature

1/2 cup granulated sugar

2 large eggs, room temperature

1 tablespoon all-purpose flour

1/4 cup heavy cream

2 teaspoons pure vanilla extract

8 whole Oreo cookies, coarsely chopped

For the Topping

1 cup whipped cream or whipped topping

8 whole Oreo cookies, coarsely chopped

chocolate sauce, optional

DIRECTIONS

Tightly wrap the bottom of 7-inch spring form pan in foil and spray the inside of the pan with non-stick cooking spray.

In a small bowl, stir together the 12 crushed Oreo cookies and melted butter and press the crumbs into the bottom of the prepared pan.

Place pan in freezer for 10-15 minutes.

In the bowl of your stand mixer fitted with the paddle attachment, or in a large bowl with an electric mixer, beat the cream cheese until smooth. Add sugar and mix until combined. Add eggs, one at a time, fully incorporating each before adding the next. Making sure to scrape down the bowl in between each egg. Add in the flour, heavy cream, and vanilla and mix until smooth. Fold in 8 chopped Oreo cookies and pour batter into prepared pan.

Cover the top of the pan with a piece of foil.

Pour 1 1/2 cups of water into the Instant Pot and place the trivet in the bottom of the pot.

Create a "foil sling" by folding a 20-inch long piece of foil in half lengthwise two times. This "sling" will allow you place and remove the springform pan with ease.

Place the cheesecake pan in the center of the sling and carefully lower the pan into the Instant Pot. Fold down the excess foil from the sling to ensure the pot closes properly.

Lock the lid into place and make sure the vent is closed "sealing". Press the "Manual" button and cook on high pressure for 40 minutes.

When the Instant Pot beeps, hit the "Keep Warm/Cancel" button to turn off the pressure cooker. Allow the pressure to release naturally for 10 minutes and then do a quick release to release any pressure remaining in the pot.

Carefully unfold the foil sling and remove the cheesecake from the pot to a cooling rack using the foil sling "handles". Uncover the cheesecake and allow it to cool to room temperature.

Once the cheesecake has cooled, refrigerate it for at least 8 hours, or overnight.

Before serving, top with whipped cream, chopped Oreo cookies, and a drizzle of chocolate sauce.

Banana Chocolate Bundt Cake

Total Time: 35 mins

Servings: 6

INGREDIENTS

1 1/2 C. Organic All Purpose, Unbleached Flour

2 Bananas, ripe

1/4 C. Raw Honey

1 tsp Vanilla

2 Eggs

3 Tbsp Coconut Oil

1/2 C. Milk + 1 Tbsp Milk

1Tbsp Vinegar

1 tsp Baking Soda

2 drops Nutmeg Essential Oil

1/2 tsp Cinnamon

1/3 C. Chocolate Chips

DIRECTIONS

Spray your 3 C. bundt pan generously with baking spray OR, grease using butter and lightly flour inside. Set aside.

Add the vinegar to the milk and let sit until it starts to curdle and turn into buttermilk.

Mix the bananas, honey, vanilla, eggs, oil, milk, buttermilk and nutmeg essential oil and blend on high until combined.

Stir in the dry ingredients (flour, cinnamon, baking soda).

Fold in the chocolate chips.

Pour the batter into the bundt pan, and shake to distribute evenly.

Place the trivet in the Instant Pot along with 2/3 C. water.

Take the bundt pan and place it atop the trivet.

Lock the lid on the Instant Pot, close the valve, and set the timer for 25 minutes on high (manual).

Once the IP beeps, do a quick release, and carefully remove the bundt pan - you may see some condensation on top of the cake and that is O.K. - it will go away once the cake cools.

Cool for 10 minutes and then carefully remove from the pan and finish cooling before slicing.

Dust the cooled cake with a light layer of powdered sugar for presentation.

Blueberry Pudding

Total Time: 50 mins

Servings: 1-2

INGREDIENTS

1 cup plain flour

1-1/2 tsp baking powder

1/2 tsp salt

1/2 cup butter, cut into small pieces, plus extra for greasing

2-1/2 tbsp dried breadcrumbs

1/2 cup granulated sugar

1 egg, beaten

5 oz. milk

1/2 lb. blueberries

Crème fraîche or cream, to serve

DIRECTIONS

Butter a 4-6 cup pudding basin.

Sift the flour, baking powder and salt into a large bowl. Mix in the butter using two knives, then add the breadcrumbs and sugar, and mix well. Finally, stir in the egg and milk, blend well, then gently stir in the blueberries.

Pour the mixture into your prepared basin, filling only 3/4 of the basin to allow room to rise.

Take a double square of parchment paper, large enough to hang over the rim of the basin by an inch or so, and fold a pleat into it to allow for expansion. Butter the underside, and secure the paper with a long piece of string under the rim. Loop the string over the basin and tie on the opposite side to make a handle.

Heat up at least 2" water in your instant pot with the steamer insert (or an improvised steamer rack) in place. Put the basin into the steamer, cover the instant pot without clamping the lid closed, and steam for 15 minutes. This is essential to allow the sponge to rise.

Now clamp on the lid. Bring up to full pressure, turn the heat down to medium and cook for 35 minutes.

Turn off the heat and vent immediately. Remove the basin using the string handle. Run a knife around the inside of the basin and turn out onto a plate. Serve with crème fraîche or cream if you wish.

Peanut Butter Cheesecake

Total Time: 18 mins

Servings: 8

INGREDIENTS

16 ounces cream cheese

2 eggs

2 tablespoons powdered peanut butter

1 tablespoon cocoa

1 teaspoon vanilla extract

1/2 cup Swerve sugar substitute

DIRECTIONS

Make sure all ingredients are at room temperature. Add cream cheese and eggs into your blender and blend until smooth. Then add additional ingredients, blending to incorporate together.

Once blended, add to 4 or 8-ounce mason jars and cover with foil or the Mason jar lid.

Add 1 cup of water to your Instant Pot and insert trivet.

Place jars inside Instant Pot and cook in 2 batches (I could only get 2 8-ounce jars or 4 4 ounce jars in at one time).

Cook on High pressure for 15-18 minutes. Let it naturally release and chill for a few hours up to overnight.

Top with whipped heavy cream and a drizzle of peanut butter or a few chopped peanuts for some texture.

Samoa Cheesecake

Total Time: 3 hrs 20 mins

Servings: 1-2

INGREDIENTS

16 oz Ricotta cheese

16 oz cream cheese

8 oz sour cream

4 eggs

2 tbs corn starch

2 tbs flour

1 tbs vanilla extract

2 cups crumbled Oreos

2 7" springform pans

For the Topping:

1 can sweetened condensed milk

1 cup melted chocolate

1 cup shredded coconut

DIRECTIONS

Mix together cream cheese, ricotta cheese. Add in eggs one at a time.

Add in flour and corn starch. Fold in sour cream.

Add crushed Oreos to the bottom of your spring form pan.

Pour your mixture into the pan. Place foil around your pan to make it easier to remove from the instant pot.

Place 1 cup of water in your instant pot. Place cheesecake on the trivet. Cook on manual high pressure for 40 minutes.

Do a quick release.

Remove cheesecake and set aside to cool for 1-2 hours.

For the topping: Place one can of condensed milk into the instant pot laying down on the trivet Completely cover the pan with water.

Cook on high pressure for 40 minutes. Do a quick release and let cool.

Remove can and let completely cool open can and spread caramel over your cheesecake.

Coat with coconut and melted chocolate.

Apple Upside-Down Cake

Total Time: 35 mins

Servings: 6

INGREDIENTS

Special equipment needed: Instant Pot, 7 x 2 inch round aluminum cake pan, parchment paper, aluminum foil.

2 cups water

4 small Gala apples, peeled and cut into ¼-inch slices

2 tablespoons lemon juice

½ teaspoon dried lavender flowers

½ cup tigernut flour

1/3 cup cassava flour

2 tablespoons coconut flour

½ teaspoon baking powder

Pinch fine sea salt

1/3 cup palm shortening, melted

3 tablespoons maple syrup

1 teaspoon vanilla extract

1 tablespoon gelatin powder

DIRECTIONS

Add water to the Instant Pot and insert the steaming basket in the pot. Line the bottom of the cake pan with parchment paper.

In a dish, mix apples, lemon juice, and lavender together. Spread apples evenly in the bottom of the cake pan.

In a large bowl, combine tigernut flour, cassava flour, coconut flour, and baking powder, salt.

In a separate bowl, mix together palm shortening, maple syrup, and vanilla extract. Stir well.

Sprinkle gelatin powder over palm shortening mixture and whisk vigorously until well blended.

Pour liquid mixture over dry ingredients and mix well with a spatula to form a ball of dough.

Transfer dough to a piece of parchment paper and flatten with your finger to form a circle no bigger than the cake pan.

Cover apples with dough and discard the parchment paper.

Cover the cake pan with a piece of aluminum foil, tucking it in all around the rim to create a tight seal.

Place the cake pan in the steaming basket. Close and lock the lid. Press "manual" and cook on high pressure for 25 minutes.

When time is up, press cancel and let the pressure release naturally before opening the lid.

You can serve this apple tea cake hot or cold.

To serve, turn the cake pan upside down and unmold on a serving platter. Eat as is or with a scoop of vanilla ice cream.

Chocolate Cake

Total Time: 20 mins

Servings: 1-2

INGREDIENTS

1 green plantain

1/2 ripe banana

1/4 cup mashed avocado

2 TB melted coconut oil, plus additional for greasing pans

2 TB honey

5 TB carob powder

1/2 tsp apple cider vinegar

3/4 tsp baking soda

1/8 tsp cream of tartar

1 cup water

Optional garnishes: coconut cream, coconut flakes, or fruit

DIRECTIONS

Add the plantain, banana, avocado, coconut oil, honey, carob, vinegar, baking soda, and cream of tartar to a food processor and blend until smooth

Lightly grease three mini fluted pans or ramekins with additional coconut oil. Pour the batter into prepared pans until they are about ¾ of the way full.

Pour the water into the Instant Pot and add the steaming rack. Place the pans onto the steaming rack.

Close and lock the lid. Press MANUAL for high pressure. Set cooking time to 18 minutes. Once time is up, quick release the pressure by carefully flipping the valve on the lid

Garnish with coconut cream, coconut flakes, or fruit and serve warm.

Pumpkin Pudding

Total Time: 30 mins

Servings: 5

INGREDIENTS

For the pumpkin pudding:

½ cup coconut milk (raw milk is also fine if you tolerate dairy)

2 teaspoons sustainably-sourced gelatin

¾ cup packed pumpkin (or well-drained homemade pumpkin puree)

½ cup coconut sugar

1 pastured egg

1 teaspoon ground cinnamon

½ teaspoon ground nutmeg

½ teaspoon ground ginger

¼ teaspoon ground cloves

½ teaspoon allspice

½ teaspoon sea salt

1 cup water

For the coconut-ginger glaze:

¾ cup coconut cream, at room temperature

1 teaspoon ground ginger

1/16 teaspoon stevia

Directions

Add milk to a saucepan.

Then sprinkle with gelatin.

Turn heat to medium-low to gently heat the milk.

Whisk the milk to dissolve the gelatin.

Then remove from heat.

In a medium size mixing bowl, combine the milk + gelatin, pumpkin, coconut sugar, egg, spices, and salt.

Whisk until smooth.

Then pour into a well-greased 3-cup bowl, soufflé dish, or Jell-O mold.

Add 1 cup water and trivet to instant pot.

Place the pumpkin pudding on the trivet.

Then put on the lid of your cooker, checking that the seals and all components are in good shape, including being in the sealing position.

Set Instant Pot to high pressure for 30 minutes.

Then once cycle is complete, hit the Cancel button to turn off the heat.

Place a towel over the pressure release knob and allow pot to do a quick pressure release.

Then carefully remove the pudding and allow it to cool to room temperature. Do not disturb it while it cools.

Next, put the pudding into the refrigerator for 4 to 6 hours, or until it is totally set.

Run a butter knife around the edge of the cooking dish and turn the pudding over on to a plate or cake stand.

Combine the glaze ingredients by whisking in a small bowl until completely smooth.

Then drizzle over the finished pudding.

Finally, garnish with crispy walnuts, if desired. Enjoy!

Chocolate Pudding Cake

Total Time: 11 mins

Servings: 4

INGREDIENTS

2/3 C semi-sweet chocolate morsels

1/2 C applesauce

2 eggs

1 tsp vanilla

pinch of salt

1/4 C arrowroot

3 Tbsp cocoa powder (plus more for dusting)

powdered sugar for topping (optional)

DIRECTIONS

Place a trivet inside the Instant Pot and pour in 2 cups of water. Measure the chocolate morsels into a heatproof ramekin, and set on the trivet. Turn the IP on to sauté, and melt the chocolate over the simmering water. Remove ramekin from IP once the chocolate is melted.

Combine the applesauce, eggs, and vanilla in a small mixing bowl. Whisk until well blended. Add the dry ingredients (salt through cocoa powder) and slowly mix in until no dry streaks remain. Stir in melted chocolate.

Liberally grease a 6" cake pan with butter or coconut oil. Dust the bottom and sides of the cake pan with cocoa powder. Pour in the cake batter, and set the pan on the trivet above the hot water in the IP.

Cook on high pressure for 4 minutes. Quick release pressure when timer goes off. Remove the cake pan from IP and let cool 10 minutes before transferring to a serving plate. Dust with powdered sugar (optional).

Chocolate Lava Cake

Total Time: 35 mins

Servings: 4

INGREDIENTS

1 Tbsp granulated sugar

1/2 cup butter, cut into pieces

4 oz semisweet chocolate, chopped

1 cup confectioners' sugar

2 eggs

2 egg yolks

1 tsp instant coffee granules

1 tsp vanilla extract

6 Tbsp all purpose flour

1/4 tsp salt

DIRECTIONS

Grease the bottom and sides of four 6 oz ramekins. Coat each with sugar.

Melt chocolate and butter: In a medium-sized microwave-safe bowl, microwave butter and chocolate for about 1 minute on medium power. Stir and repeat heating at 15-second intervals, until the chocolate is melted and smooth.

Stir in confectioner's sugar.

Whisk in eggs, yolks, coffee and vanilla.

Stir in flour and salt.

Divide batter among the ramekins.

Pour 2 cups water into the Instant Pot's main compartment (inner pot) and place trivet in water.

Place 3 ramekins on the trivet and place 1 more on top of them, in the middle (staggered). Close the Instant Pot. Make sure the steam release handle is in the 'Sealing' position.

Cook on 'Manual' for 9 minutes.

Do a Quick Release of steam and open the Instant Pot.

Use the trivet to remove the ramekins. Gently dab off any condensation from the surface of the cake.

Dust the Instant Pot chocolate lava cakes with powdered sugar.

Serve warm and enjoy!

Peppermint Cheesecake

Total Time: 45 mins

Servings: 8-10

INGREDIENTS

16 ounces full fat organic cultured cream cheese, softened

2 pastured or organic eggs, room temperature

1/2 cup maple sugar

1/4 cup organic cultured sour cream {preferably grass-fed}

1 tablespoon Otto's cassava flour

1 1/2 teaspoons vanilla extract

1/4 teaspoon peppermint extract

1/2 teaspoon sea salt

For the Crust:

1 cup blanched almond flour

2 tablespoons maple sugar

2 tablespoons melted grass-fed butter or ghee, melted

For the Chocolate Ganache:

6 ounces allergy-friendly chocolate, chopped

1/3 cup organic cream

1/4 teaspoon sea salt

Flaked sea salt for sprinkling on top of the ganache

DIRECTIONS

Get your springform pan ready and set aside. Add almond flour, maple sugar and melted butter/ghee to a small bowl. With clean hands, mix until completely combined. Dump mixture into your springform pan and press down forming a packed "crust" at the bottom {don't allow too much to go up the sides}. Place springform pan in the freezer for 10 minutes.

While the springform pan is in the freezer, prepare the cheesecake filling. Add all cheesecake filling ingredients to a high powdered blender and blend on low speed until smooth and combined. Pour cheesecake filling into the frozen springform mold.

Use a spoon or spatula to evenly distribute and smooth the top. Place Instant Pot trivet in your Instant Pot. Add 1 cup water to the Instant Pot.

Gently place your springform pan in the Instant Pot and cover with glass lid. Secure your Instant Pot lid making sure the seal valve is closed.

Press Manual {High Pressure} and increase the time of 35 minutes. Walk away. When the cook time is done, press the cancel button to turn off the Instant Pot. Unplug your Instant Pot and let it naturally pressure release for 15 minutes.

Using an oven mitt, release the seal valve letting any remaining pressure out. Remove the lid and carefully lift trivet and cheesecake out of the Instant Pot {please use CAUTION doing this, use oven mitts or thick towels, the Instant Pot and springform pan will be extremely HOT}. Allow to cool to room temperature with the lid remaining on.

Once cooled, remove the lid taking care not to drip any of the condensation on the top of the cheesecake and gently run a knife around the edges of the cheesecake. This will help loosen the cheesecake when you're ready to remove it from the outer springform.

Wipe off all condensation from the lid and place back on top of the cheesecake and place in the refrigerator for at least 4 hours until completely chilled, best overnight.

When the cheesecake is chilled, make chocolate ganache. Place cream in a small saucepan and bring to a boil. Immediately remove from heat and add chopped chocolate and sea salt. Stir until all chocolate is melted and it's smooth and shiny.

Pour over the top of the cheesecake. Use a spoon to smooth out the ganache and sprinkle the top with flaked sea salt.

Greek Yogurt Cheesecake

Total Time: 35 mins

Servings: 8

INGREDIENTS

6 oz. graham crackers

4 tablespoons unsalted butter, melted

4 oz. regular (not low-fat) cream cheese, softened

1 1/2 cups whole milk Greek yogurt

1/4 cup sugar

1 teaspoon vanilla

2 large eggs

DIRECTIONS

Start with the crust: crush the cookies/crackers into fine crumbs, using either a food processor or a ziploc bag to crumble by hand. Stir in the melted butter, then press the mixture onto the bottom of a 7-inch springform pan, pressing firmly and spreading the crust about halfway up the sides of the pan (the bottom of a drinking glass works well for this job).

Combine the softened cream cheese, Greek yogurt, sugar and vanilla in a large bowl, and whip together until very smooth. Then add the eggs, one at a time, mixing until just combined.

Pour the filling into the springform pan, being careful to fully cover the crust around the edges (if any crumbs are exposed, they can become soggy from the moisture in the pressure cooker).

Place a trivet rack into the pressure cooker, and pour in 1 cup of water. Place the cheesecake on top of the trivet and close the lid. Set the valve to sealing position, and cook on high pressure for 30 minutes (on the Instant Pot, select "Manual" and use the default setting).

After the cooking time is up and the pressure has released naturally, open the lid and use the trivet handles to lift out the pan. If water has settled on top of the cheesecake, gently blot any excess with a paper towel. Allow the cheesecake to cool on a rack at room temperature for 1-2 hours, then transfer it to the refrigerator to chill completely (at least 4 hours).

Maple Flan

Total Time: 1 hr. 25 mins

Servings: 8

INGREDIENTS

½ cup + ¼ cup maple syrup

3 large eggs + 4 large egg yolks

1½ cup whole milk

1½ cup heavy cream (not ultra-pasteurized)

½ teaspoon sea salt

1 tablespoon vanilla extract

DIRECTIONS

Place trivet in instant pot.

Add 3½ cups water into cooker.

If using an electric instant pot, set to Sauté function so water will heat up.

Place a 7.25-inch souffle dish inside instant pot on trivet.

Cover instant pot or crockpot with lid to prevent evaporation.

In a small saucepan, bring ½ cup maple syrup to simmer.

Cook over medium heat until syrup starts to smell slightly burnt (8 to 10 minutes).

Pour syrup into souffle dish. It should cover the entire bottom.

Whisk and eggs and egg yolks with remaining ¼ cup of maple syrup.

Combine milk, cream, salt, and vanilla in a medium saucepan.

Heat slightly until it just starts to steam.

While whisking constantly, very slowly pour warm milk/cream mixture into egg mixture.

Strain through a fine mesh strainer into souffle dish, on top of maple syrup already inside.

Cover instant pot or crockpot with lid. If using a instant pot, leave the sealing valve open so it can vent.

Let steam for 1 hour and 15 minutes or until center of custard jiggles slightly when shaken and internal temperature is 180 degrees Fahrenheit.

Remove lid.

Transfer inner pot of instant pot or crockpot to a wire rack, with the souffle dish still inside, and allow cooling for 1 hour.

Carefully lift out souffle dish.

Cover and refrigerate until completely cold.

To unmold, run a knife or a wooden stick around edges of the dish.

Invert serving platter on top of the souffle dish, and then turn the dish and the platter over.

Lavender Crème Brûlée

Total Time: 25 mins

Servings: 1

INGREDIENTS

1 Egg Yolk from a free range pastured chicken egg.

1/3 C Heavy Cream

1 tsp Raw Sugar

1 tsp Vanilla Extract

Tiny bits of real vanilla beans

Pinch of food grade organic lavender buds

1 tsp of raw sugar for topping

DIRECTIONS

Warm heavy cream and dissolve sugar and then cool to room temp

Whisk egg yolk into the cream mixture.

Add vanilla extract, vanilla bean and lavender buds.

Pour into a ramekin.

Add 1 cup water and place the trivet or a steamer.

Place the ramekin on top of the trivet.

Set on HIGH for 9 minutes and NPR

Take out the ramekin and cool for at least 45 minutes and refrigerate for additional 4- 5 hours or overnight.

Sprinkle 1 tsp of sugar and broil until the sugar browns. Be careful not to broil it too long as it will make the crème get softer. If it happens, put it back in the fridge until it gets firmer.

Bread Pudding

Total Time: 40 mins

Servings: 10-12

INGREDIENTS

1 loaf bread grain-free, sourdough, gluten-free

2 cups milk preferably raw or high-fat coconut

4 whole eggs

1/2 cup pure maple syrup

1/2 cup butter or preferred traditional fat, melted

2 egg yolks

1 Tablespoon real vanilla extract

1/4 teaspoon sea salt

DIRECTIONS

Cut bread into 1" cubes. Select bowl that will fit into the Instant Pot's stainless steel inner pot. I used a metal bowl with sloping sides that is about 4" high and 7-1/2" wide across the top. Place a piece of parchment paper into the bowl, pressing flat any folds. Add cubes to lined bowl.

Place the following items into blender: milk, eggs, yolks, maple syrup, vanilla and sea salt. Blend for 10-15 seconds, then, with motor still running, add melted butter through the door in lid.

Add 2 cups water to Instant Pot's stainless steel inner pot. Place trivet into Instant Pot. Place bowl with bread on top. Pour custard into bowl, pressing on bread gently so as to wet all the cubes. Place a small square of parchment paper over the surface of the pudding, and fold in any corners from the bottom piece that may be sticking out.

Place lid on IP. Seal and close vent. Press Steam button and adjust the time to 15 minutes. When timer goes off, allow the pressure to release on its own for 20 minutes; then press Cancel button and open pot.

Allow bowl to cool slightly, and then remove pudding by lifting up on the corners of parchment that line the bowl. Transfer to a plate and flip over, so the bottom is the top. Slice and serve, with optional caramelized pears. Whipped cream would also be a lovely accompaniment.

Chocolate Zucchini Bites

Total Time: 38 mins

Servings: 10-12

INGREDIENTS

2 eggs

¾ to 1 cup evaporated cane juice

½ cup coconut oil

2 teaspoons vanilla extract

1 tablespoon butter, melted

3 tablespoons cocoa powder

1 cup sprouted einkorn flour (learn how to sprout your grains)

½ teaspoon baking soda

¼ teaspoon sea salt

¾ teaspoon cinnamon

1 cups zucchini (or squash), grated

1/3 cup chocolate chips or chocolate chunks

1 cup water

DIRECTIONS

Combine eggs, sweetener, coconut oil, and vanilla extract in a medium-sized mixing bowl.

Stir well.

Next, add cocoa powder to melted butter.

Mix until it looks like a thick but smooth dark paste.

Then, add chocolate mixture to egg mixture and stir well.

Add flour, baking soda, sea salt, and cinnamon to the bowl.

Stir well.

Fold in grated zucchini and chocolate chips.

Then, add trivet and 1 cup of water to the inner pot of your Instant Pot or other pressure cooker.

Cover with a glass lid to prevent evaporation.

If using an electric cooker (such as the Instant Pot), put it on sauté so it can pre-heat.

Using a small cookie scoop, fill silicone muffin cups about 2/3 full. The 6-quart Instant Pot fits 16 muffin cups at a time. This means you'll have batter left over. Either pressure cook these muffins after the first batch is done, or cook them in the oven at the same.

Then, layer muffin cups inside inner pot of instant pot.

Once bottom layer is full, cover with piece of parchment paper and piece of aluminum foil. Both should be cut in a circle to the size of the inner pot.

Cover with a plate or another trivet.

Then put the rest of the muffin cups inside to fill up the second layer. Try to keep all the muffin cups level!

Again, cover with parchment paper and aluminum foil, then a plate.

Cover the instant pot, checking that the seal and other parts are in good shape.

If using an electric cooker, set to high for 8 minutes.

When cooking time is over, if using an electric cooker, let it sit for 10 to 15 minutes while it depressurizes naturally.

Then, if any pressure remains, cover release valve with a towel and quick release.

Next check for doneness with a toothpick.

Finally, carefully unpack your lovely, moist chocolate-y muffins!

For special occasions (or just for fun), top your pressure cooker muffins with this chocolate cream cheese frosting!

Lemongrass and Coconut Chicken

Total Time: 20 mins

Servings: 4

INGREDIENTS

1 thick stalk fresh lemongrass, papery outer skins and rough bottom removed, trimmed to the bottom 5 inches

4 cloves garlic, peeled and crushed

1 thumb-size piece of ginger, peeled and roughly chopped

2 tablespoons Red Boat fish sauce

3 tablespoons coconut aminos

1 teaspoon five spice powder

1 cup full-fat coconut milk (+¼ cup optional)

10 drumsticks, skin removed

1 teaspoon Diamond Crystal kosher salt

½ teaspoon freshly ground black pepper

1 teaspoon ghee or coconut oil

1 large onion, peeled and thinly sliced

¼ cup fresh cilantro, chopped

Juice from 1 lime (optional)

DIRECTIONS

Peel, trim, and smash the piece of lemongrass.

Combine the lemongrass, garlic, ginger, fish sauce, coconut aminos, and five-spice powder into a blender or food processor. Pour in the coconut milk and blitz until a smooth sauce forms.

Remove the skin from the drum sticks.

Put the chicken drumsticks into a large bowl and season with salt and pepper. Toss the chicken with the salt and pepper.

Press the "Sauté" button on the Instant Pot to heat up the insert.

Add a teaspoon of ghee or coconut oil. Once it melts, add sliced onions. Fry the onions until they are translucent.

Add the drumsticks to the pot and pour the marinade on top. Press the "Cancel/Warm" button on the Instant Pot and lock the lid with the top dial pointed towards the sealed position.

Press the "Manual" or "Pressure Cook" button and set it to cook for 15 minutes under high pressure.

When the stew finishes cooking, turn off the pressure heater (or turn off the heat) and release the pressure valve. Once the pressure drops, unlock the lid and taste for seasoning.

Lemon Mustard Chicken and Potatoes

Total Time: 20 mins

Servings: 1-2

INGREDIENTS

2 Tbsp Olive Oil

3/4 c. chicken broth

1/4 c. lemon juice

2 lb chicken thighs

2-3 Tbsp Dijon mustard

2 Tbsp Italian Seasoning

2-3 pounds red potatoes, quartered

Salt and pepper

DIRECTIONS

Add oil to Instant Pot

Salt and pepper chicken thighs to taste and add to Instant Pot.

Combine chicken broth, lemon juice, and Dijon mustard, mix well and pour over chicken.

Add quartered potatoes and Italian Seasoning

Place lid on Instant Pot and cook on MANUAL for 15 minutes

Quick Release at end of 15-minutes.

Chicken Cacciatore Recipe

Total Time: 20 mins

Servings: 4

INGREDIENTS

4 tablespoons butter

1 pound chicken legs

½ pound boneless chicken thighs

½ teaspoon salt

½ teaspoon black pepper

½ onion, minced

½ red bell pepper, finely diced

1 cup mushrooms, sliced

2 cloves garlic, minced

1 tablespoon capers, drained

1 14.5-ounce can diced tomatoes

1 cup chicken broth or water

1 tablespoon fresh basil leaves, rough chopped

DIRECTIONS

Season chicken parts with salt and pepper.

Use the Sauté setting on the Instant Pot to brown the chicken with 2 Tbsp of the butter until the chicken until golden brown, about 3 minutes on each side. Remove the chicken from the pot and set aside.

Add the remaining 2 tablespoons of butter, onions, and peppers and sauté for 2 to 3 minutes until the onion becomes translucent. Add the mushrooms and continue to cook, stirring for 2 minutes. Add the garlic and stir until aromatic, about 1 minute. Add the capers and diced tomatoes.

Add the mushrooms and continue to cook, stirring for 2 minutes. Add the garlic and stir until aromatic, about 1 minute. Add the capers and diced tomatoes.

Add the garlic and stir until aromatic, about 1 minute. Add the capers and diced tomatoes.

Add the capers and diced tomatoes.

Retun the chicken to the pot and cover everything with the chicken broth or water.

Close the lid.

Press "Poultry".

Allow Natural Pressure Release for 10-minutes.

Moana Shredded Chicken

Total Time: 20 mins

Servings: 2-4

INGREDIENTS

6 skinless, boneless chicken breasts

12 ounce can of frozen orange juice concentrate

1 Tablespoons lemon juice

1 teaspoon soy sauce

15.25 ounce can of peaches in juice

20 ounce can of pineapple chunks in juice

¼ cup brown sugar

1 Tablespoon cornstarch

1 Tablespoon water

hamburger buns or rice

DIRECTIONS

In the Instant Pot mix orange juice concentrate, lemon juice, soy sauce, peaches, pineapple chunks and brown sugar.

Stir until brown sugar is completely dissolved.

Place chicken breasts into the sauce.

Place lid on Instant Pot and lock into place, making sure valve is turned to closed (to build pressure).

Set Instant Pot on Manual for 12-minutes.

Release pressure valve and allow all pressure to release then open Instant Pot.

Remove chicken.

Mix 1 Tablespoon cornstarch with 1 Tablespoon water (or sauce) in a small mixing bowl until well blended and no lumps.

Turn Instant Pot to Sauté and pour cornstarch mixture into sauce, stirring until well mixed. Allow sauce to boil, while stirring occasionally until thickened.

While sauce is thickening, shred the chicken. I use two forks, but do whatever works best for you.

Now it's time to make a decision.

You can either serve the chicken and drizzle the sauce over it, or you can add the shredded chicken into the sauce in the Instant Pot.

Creamy Chicken Alfredo Pasta

Total Time: 20 mins

Servings: 1-2

INGREDIENTS

16 oz. pasta

16 oz. Asiago Cheese

a pint of Heavy Cream

1 cup white wine

2 cups water

2 cloves garlic

1 Tbsp oil

8 oz. sliced mushrooms

1 Tbsp flour

16 oz frozen broccoli

1 lb. boneless, skinless chicken breast, cut into cubes

DIRECTIONS

Set Instant Pot to Sauté setting.

Add olive oil and minced garlic.

Stir garlic for 2 minutes and then add chicken chunks.

Sauté chicken until almost done, about 4 minutes.

Add white wine.

Add pasta and 2 cups of water. You may need to add more water--you want to "just cover" the pasta.

Add broccoli to the top.

Add mushrooms.

Place lid on Instant pot and place on high on the manual setting for 8-minutes.

Perform a quick release.

Check noodles, if they aren't as soft as you like, add another two minutes.

Pour in heavy cream and stir.

Stir in flour.

Turn Instant Pot on to Sauté and stir until sauce thickens.

As soon as it begins to thicken, shut down the unit.

Add cheese.

Stir and serve.

Chicken, Mushrooms and Artichoke Hearts

Total Time: 20 mins

Servings: 1-2

INGREDIENTS

2 Tbsp Olive Oil

salt and pepper to taste

4 chicken breasts

1 leek, quartered and sliced

1 lb fresh, whole mushrooms

1 can (28 ounces) Tuttorosso Tomatoes

1 jar artichoke hearts

¾ cup chicken broth

1 bag fresh baby spinach

DIRECTIONS

Add olive oil to bottom of Instant Pot

Salt and Pepper chicken breasts to your liking

Add chicken to bottom of Instant Pot

Add mushrooms and leek

Drain Tuttorosso Tomatoes and add to Instant Pot

Drain Artichoke Hearts and add to Instant Pot

Pour in chicken broth

top with baby spinach

Put the lid on the Instant Pot and set for Poultry 20-minutes.

Salsa Shredded Chicken

Total Time: 20 mins

Servings: 5

INGREDIENTS

1 pound skinless, boneless chicken breast

1/2 teaspoon kosher salt

3/4 teaspoon cumin

black pepper, to taste

pinch oregano

1 cup chunky salsa

DIRECTIONS

Season chicken on both sides with spices.

Place into the Instant Pot and cover with salsa.

Cover and press the "poultry" button then add 5 minutes to cook the chicken for a total of 20 minutes.

Once the Instant Pot releases the pressure, put the chicken onto a plate and use two forks to shred.

Sticky Chicken

Total Time: 50 mins

Servings: 2

INGREDIENTS

1 lb. chicken drumsticks (about 6)

1 tsp. paprika

1 tsp. garlic powder

1 tsp. ground cumin

½ tsp. ground ginger

½ tsp. ground cinnamon

¼ tsp. ground coriander

¼ tsp. packed saffron threads

1 tsp. sea salt

½ tsp. black pepper

½ c. bone broth or stock of choice

¼ c. honey

2 tsp. blackstrap molasses

1 medium lemon, zest & juice

Optional for garnish: sesame seeds, chopped scallions

DIRECTIONS

Pat the chicken dry with paper towels. Make the spice rub by combining the paprika, garlic powder, cumin, ginger, cinnamon, coriander, saffron (crush it into small pieces between two hands or with a mortar & pestle), sea salt, and black pepper. Coat the chicken with the rub well on all sides.

Set the Instant Pot to "Sauté" with the lid off. When it reads "Hot," grease the bottom with a small amount of avocado oil, ghee, or lard. Brown the drumsticks on all sides, about 15 minutes in total.

Add the broth to the pot. Turn the Instant Pot to "Keep Warm/Cancel" and put the lid on. Set to "Manual" and move the time to 10 minutes. Make sure the steam valve is set to "Sealing," as we are using pressure to cook the drumsticks.

After the drumsticks have finished, press the "Keep Warm/Cancel" to turn it off. Release the pressure by moving the steam valve to "Venting." Always use caution as the steam is hot. Note: do not use the optional natural steam release here, as it can cause the chicken to continue to overcook and become dry.

Remove the lid and with tongs, carefully move the chicken (it may be falling off the bone) to a large bowl and cover it tightly with foil to keep warm. Leave the juices rendered from the cooking process in the pan. Turn the Instant Pot to "Sauté" again and keep the lid off.

In a small bowl, whisk together the honey, molasses, lemon juice and zest. Pour into the pot with the reserved cooking juices. When the indicator hits "Hot," you should have a rolling boil. Whisk occasionally (being cautious of the steam) until the liquid has reduced to a thick sauce, about 5-10 minutes. If you accidentally let it go too long, it'll get too thick and sticky to use. Simply add a couple of tablespoons of water and whisk to smooth it out.

Coat the drumsticks with the sauce. Serve garnished with sesame seeds and chopped scallions, as desired.

Polynesian Chicken

Total Time: 20 mins

Servings: 8

INGREDIENTS

6 boneless, skinless chicken breasts

1 (12 ounce) can frozen orange juice concentrate

2 Tablespoons lemon juice

1 teaspoon soy sauce

1 (15.25 ounce) can peaches, with juice

1 (20 ounce) can pineapple chunks, with juice

1/4 cup light brown sugar

1 Tablespoon cornstarch

Hamburger Buns

Fresh sliced pineapple, grilled

DIRECTIONS

In a bowl mix orange juice concentrate, lemon juice, soy sauce, peaches, pineapple chunks & brown sugar.

Pour 1/2 mixture into instant pot.

Place chicken breasts on top of sauce.

Pour remaining sauce over chicken.

Lock lid into place.

Press Instant Pot Feature

Cook for 12 minutes with pressure valve closed.

When pot is finished, carefully open pressure valve and allow pressure to release.

Once pressure has been released, open pot, remove chicken and shred.

Strain juice from instant pot into a pot.

Remove one Tablespoon of juice and put into a small bowl.

Add 1 Tablespoon of cornstarch and mix well.

Add cornstarch mixture to juice.

Cook over medium heat until juice mixture thickens.

Pour over shredded chicken, toss to coat.

Place 1/4 cup of shredded chicken mixture onto a hamburger bun.

Top with grilled pineapple slice and devour.

Honey Bourbon Chicken

Total Time: 10 mins

Servings: 4

INGREDIENTS

1 ½ pounds Chicken, Thighs, Boneless/Skinless

1/8 teaspoons Salt

1/8 teaspoons Black Pepper

½ cups dice Onion

½ cups Soy Sauce

¼ cups Ketchup

2 tablespoons Vegetable Oil

2 teaspoons mince Garlic, Cloves

¼ tablespoons Red Pepper Flakes

1 cup Honey

DIRECTIONS

Due to the nature of pressure cooking there is always room for inconsistency. The times given here are based on 4 servings fresh. If you are using more servings you may need to increase your cooking time.

Place all ingredients except for cornstarch and water into inner pot.

Lock cover into place and seal steam nozzle.

Cook on the chicken setting or manually set for 15 minutes. If you are using frozen chicken, add an additional 10 minutes.

Naturally release pressure for 5 minutes then quick release remaining pressure.

Remove chicken and dice.

Set Instant Pot setting to Sauté.

In a bowl, combine cornstarch and water.

Add cornstarch mixture and chicken to pot and continue to cook for 2-3 minutes until thickened.

Rotisserie Chicken

Total Time: 45 mins

Servings: 4-6

INGREDIENTS

1 whole chicken mine was 4.3 pounds

1 and 1/2 teaspoons salt

1/2 teaspoon pepper

1 teaspoon granulated garlic

1 teaspoon paprika

1 and 3/4 Tablespoons avocado oil

1 yellow onion quartered (optional)

1 lemon halved (optional)

1 cup chicken stock or broth

DIRECTIONS

Remove all parts from the chicken cavity; rinse and pat dry with a paper towel.

Optional: place the onion and lemon in the cavity of the chicken.

Combine all of the spices, including salt and pepper, in a small ramekin dish; stir together.

Add the oil to the spices, and stir until incorporated.

Turn on your Instant Pot to preheat on the sauté setting on "normal."

Rub the oil and spice mixture on the breast side of the chicken.

Place the chicken, breast side down, in the preheated Instant Pot.

Carefully rub the other half of the oil and spices mixture on the other side of the chicken.

Allow the breast side to crisp up the chicken skin for a few minutes, about 3 to 4 minutes total.

Carefully rotate the chicken over to the other side, and let it crisp up the skin on the other side for about a minute

Add in the chicken stock.

Place the lid on and lock it, per Instant Pot instructions.

Set to manual high pressure for 25 minutes.

Allow the Instant Pot to depressurize naturally.

Remove the lid, and transfer the chicken to a serving plate.

Let the chicken rest for about 5 minutes prior to serving.

Buttery Lemon Chicken

Total Time: 20 mins

Servings: 1-2

INGREDIENTS

2 lbs. chicken breast or thighs

2 tbsp. ghee or butter

1 onion diced

¾ cup organic chicken broth

4 cloves minced garlic

1 tsp. salt

½ tsp paprika

½ tsp pepper

1 tsp. dried parsley

½ cup lemon juice (2 lemons)

4 tsp. arrowroot flour

DIRECTIONS

Set the Instant Pot to sauté mode. When it's hot melt ghee or butter.

Add onion, garlic, paprika, parsley, and pepper to melted ghee, and sauté until onions soften.

With your Instant Pot still set to sauté, sear the chicken on each side for about 3-5 minutes. The chicken should be a caramelized brown color.

Pour chicken brother, lemon juice, and salt over chicken and stir.

Lock lid into place and close steam valve. Set Instant Pot to poultry setting and cook for 7-8 mins if chicken is thawed and 12-15 minutes if it's frozen.

Once done, let depressurize naturally – it shouldn't take very long.

Remove the chicken from the Instant Pot, but leave the sauce in the pan. Gradually stir in arrowroot flour to thicken sauce.

If you're serving chicken on top pasta, mix cooked pasta in with thickened lemon sauce. Otherwise drizzle sauce over chicken.

Chicken Breasts

Total Time: 20 mins

Servings: 1-2

INGREDIENTS

1 Tablespoon oil

3 boneless, skinless chicken breasts (uncooked)

1/4 teaspoon garlic salt per chicken breast

dash black pepper

1/8 teaspoon dried oregano

1/8 teaspoon dried basil

1 cup water

DIRECTIONS

Preheat the sauté function on the Instant Pot at the highest setting, and add oil to the pot.

Season one side of the chicken breasts.

After the display reads "hot," carefully add the chicken breasts, seasoned side down, to the pot. I use tongs to avoid hot oil splatter.

Add seasoning on the second side.

Cook about 3 to 4 minutes on each side, and remove from pot with the tongs.

Add 1 cup water to the pot (may need more for 8 quart pots), plus the trivet.

Place the chicken on the trivet.

Lock the lid, and cook on manual high for 5 minutes.

Allow the chicken to naturally release for 5 minutes, and then quick release the rest.

Remove the chicken from the pot, and allow resting for about 5 minutes before serving for maximum juiciness.

Chicken Taco Bowls

Total Time: 15 mins

Servings: 6-8

INGREDIENTS

4-5 uncooked boneless, skinless chicken breasts

1-2 packets taco seasoning (1 for mild flavor, 2 for more flavor)

1 (15 oz) can black beans, drained and rinsed

1 (12 oz) bag frozen corn

1 (15.5 oz) jar salsa

3 cups uncooked jasmine rice, rinsed

3 cups water or chicken broth

cheddar cheese

cilantro (optional)

sour cream (optional)

DIRECTIONS

Place chicken breasts in bottom of instant pot. Sprinkle with taco seasoning. Top with beans and corn. Then, pour salsa over everything.

Add rice, then liquid (water or broth).

Cook on manual high pressure for 12 minutes, then use quick release to release the pressure.

Once the pressure has been fully released, remove lid carefully.

Shred chicken. Serve immediately. Top with cheddar cheese, cilantro, and sour cream as desired.

Honey Sesame Chicken

Total Time: 30 mins

Servings: 1-2

INGREDIENTS

4 boneless, skinless chicken breasts

Salt and pepper

1 cup honey

1/2 cup soy sauce

1/2 cup diced onion

1/4 cup ketchup

2 tablespoons vegetable oil

2 cloves garlic, minced

1/4 teaspoon red pepper flakes

4 teaspoons cornstarch dissolved in 6 Tablespoons water

Sesame seeds

DIRECTIONS

Place your chicken in the bottom of the Instant Pot.

In a small bowl, combine honey, soy sauce, onion, ketchup, oil, garlic and pepper flakes. Pour over chicken and put your Instant Pot Lid on and seal.

Cook on the Meat setting for 20 minutes and then quick release once the 20 minutes is up. Remove chicken from pot, leave sauce.

Dissolve 4 teaspoons of cornstarch in 6 tablespoons of water in a small bowl and pour into your Instant Pot. Stir to combine with sauce. Push the Sauté button and cook sauce for about 5 minutes or until slightly thickened.

Cut the chicken into bite size pieces, then return to pot and toss with sauce before serving. Sprinkle with sesame seeds and serve over rice or noodles.

You can also sprinkle more red pepper flakes on top if you want more heat.

Remove the Honey Sesame Chicken from the Instant Pot and put in a bowl and cook the rice in the Instant Pot. Use 2 cups of Brown Jasmine Rice and 2 cups water.

Rinse and drain 2 cups of rice and add to the Instant Pot. Add 2 cups of water. Seal your instant pot with the lid and select the Rice button. It will cook for about 10 minutes. Once finished, perform a quick release.

Chicken Burrito Bowls

Total Time: 20 mins

Servings: 4

INGREDIENTS

1 tablespoon olive oil

1 small onion, diced

1 clove garlic minced

1 teaspoon chili powder

1/2 teaspoon Kosher salt

1 1/2 pounds boneless, skinless chicken thighs, cut into 1-inch pieces

1 (15.5 ounce) can black beans, rinsed

1 cup long grain white rice uncooked

1 cup salsa

2 cups OR 1 (14.5 ounce) can chicken broth

1/4 cup chopped cilantro for serving, optional

1/4 cup grated Cheddar cheese for serving, optional

DIRECTIONS

Set electric instant pot to the Sauté setting. Heat olive oil until it shimmers but doesn't smoke. Add the onion and cook until soft, about two minutes. Add the garlic and cook an additional minute. Add chili powder and salt. Stir to combine. Add the chicken, black beans, rice, and salsa. Stir. Pour chicken broth over the mixture.

Lock the lid in place. Set a 10-minute cook time on high pressure.

Once the cook time completes, quickly release the pressure.

Open the lid away from your face. Stir with a wooden spoon or rubber spatula.

Serve with chopped cilantro and grated cheddar.

Chicken Teriyaki

Total Time: 15 mins

Servings: 3

INGREDIENTS

2 boneless skinless chicken breasts, cut in half

¼ c honey

¼ c rice wine vinegar

1 tsp ginger powder

1 Tbsp minced garlic

½ yellow onion, roughly chopped

¼ tsp pepper

2 Tbsp low sodium soy sauce

1 tsp red pepper flakes

1 Tbsp olive oil

½ Tbsp corn starch

1 Tbsp water

DIRECTIONS

Cut chicken breast in half length ways and place halves in the instant pot.

In a small bowl whisk all ingredients together except the corn starch and water.

Pour ingredients over the chicken and turn the Instant pot to high pressure and cook for five minutes.

Quick release the instant pot and check the internal temperature. Chicken should reach an internal temp of 165 degrees.

If your chicken is not fully cooked, place back in the instant pot, cover, and let sit until the temperature reached 165 degrees.

Take the chicken out of the instant pot and shred with two forks.

Turn the Instant Pot to Sauté mode and create a slurry with the corn starch and water.

Pour the slurry into the instant pot and bring the sauce to a boil. Once the sauce thickens, add shredded chicken.

Herbed Chicken

Total Time: 30 mins

Servings: 4

INGREDIENTS

2 1/2 to 3 Pound whole chicken

2 Tablespoons olive oil (divided)

sea salt & black pepper

1/2 Medium onion

5 Large cloves fresh garlic

1 teaspoon garlic powder

1 teaspoon onion powder

1 teaspoon chili powder

1 teaspoon paprika

1/2 teaspoon cumin

1/2 teaspoon basil

1 cup chicken stock or broth or water

2 Tablespoons Seasoning Mix

DIRECTIONS

Rub chicken with one Tablespoon of olive oil and sprinkle with salt and pepper.

Place the onion wedges and garlic cloves inside the chicken. Use butcher's twine to secure the legs.

Turn on the instant pot and press the Sauté button.

Add the remaining olive oil to the metal pan. When hot, add the chicken and sear/brown both sides, about 4 minutes per side.

Remove the chicken and set aside. Place the trivet at the bottom of the metal pan and add the chicken stock.

Sprinkle seasoning mix over the entire chicken, rubbing it in and spreading it around to cover the entire chicken.

Place the chicken, breast side up on top of the trivet and secure the lid. Make sure the lid is in the "Sealing" position.

Set the instant pot to Manual and set timer for 25 minutes.

When the timer beeps, allow the pressure to release naturally for 15 minutes. If the lid will not open, quick release the remaining pressure and remove the chicken.

Allow chicken to rest for 5 to 10 minutes before serving.

Thai Chicken

Total Time: 25 mins

Servings: 1

INGREDIENTS

1/3 cup reduced fat mozzarella cheese

1 whole wheat Naan

7 thinly sliced carrots

1/3th of an onion

1/3 cup kale

2 Tbsp chopped peanuts

Thai Sauce

1 Tbsp natural peanut butter

¼ tsp soy sauce

¼ tsp rice wine vinegar

Siracha sauce to taste

Red Chili Flakes to taste

Water

DIRECTIONS

To assemble your flat bread, top it with my Instant Pot Chicken, cheese, and the veggies.

Bake at 350 degrees for 10-15 minutes or until the cheese is golden brown.

While it is baking, mix together the ingredients for your sauce. You want the consistency to be similar to honey. Simply add more water if it is too thick.

Remove from the oven and top with chopped peanuts, Thai sauce, and sriracha sauce.

Delicious Shredded Chicken

Total Time: 15 mins

Servings: 4

INGREDIENTS

1 1/2 jars barbecue sauce 26 oz. or so

1 small can of chunk pineapple with juice

3 boneless / skinless chicken breasts

2 tbsp soy sauce

1 pkg. small flour tortillas

1 c shredded jack cheese

Sliced avocado – optional

DIRECTIONS

Empty 1 jar of barbecue sauce on bottom of Instant Pot (18 oz.).

Put chicken breasts on top of your sauce gently (not pushing down, you want sauce to be between pot and chicken to avoid getting too brown), squeeze half jar of 2nd jar of barbecue sauce on top of the chicken.

Empty can of pineapple with the juice on top of that, and add soy sauce.

Close Instant Pot and make sure steam valve is closed. Set to poultry setting for 15 minutes (automatically sets to this time when you hit the poultry function).

When it finishes cooking, carefully release steam valve and lift the lid.

General Tso's Chicken

Total Time: 15 mins

Servings: 1-2

INGREDIENTS

1.5 pounds cubed chicken

1 tsp Sesame Oil

6 tbsp Rice Vinegar

6 tbsp soy sauce

¼ cup Hoisin Sauce

4 tbsp Brown Sugar

2 tbsp corn starch

¼ tsp ginger

1 clove garlic chopped

¼ tsp red pepper flakes

Sesame seeds

1 chopped green onion

2 cups cooked white rice

DIRECTIONS

Place pot on Sauté.

Sauté chicken cubes in sesame oil for 1-2 minutes or until chicken is white no need to cook all the way.

In a separate bowl mix together Rice Vinegar, soy sauce, garlic, ginger, red pepper flakes, hoisin sauce, and brown sugar.

Pour mixture into the Instant pot over the chicken.

Place Manual High power for 10 minutes.

Do a quick release.

Place your pot back on Sauté bring to a slight boil and Whisk in cornstarch until mixture turns thick and bubbly about 2 minutes.

Serve over rice. Sprinkle with green onions and sesame seeds.

Apricot Chicken

Total Time: 30 mins

Servings: 1-2

INGREDIENTS

1 cup Apricot Jam

1 small bottle Russian Salad Dressing

1 package onion soup mix

5-6 chicken breasts

DIRECTIONS

Combine jam, dressing and soup mix in a bowl and mix well.

Place chicken breasts in Instant Pot, pour sauce over chicken.

Select "chicken" setting and a cook time of 30 minutes.

Serve with your favorite vegetable side.

Delicious Chicken and Rice

Total Time: 30 mins

Servings: 6

INGREDIENTS

1 pound boneless skinless chicken thighs

1 Tablespoons oil

3 small shallots diced

3 carrots diced

1 cup sliced mushrooms

2 cloves medium fresh garlic minced

1.5 cups uncooked white jasmine rice rinsed and drained

1.5 cups chicken stock or broth plus another 1/3 cup for deglazing the pan

2 Tablespoons fresh thyme leaves chopped and divided

salt and pepper to taste

DIRECTIONS

Using the sauté setting, preheat on normal for 1.5 minutes

Generously salt and pepper your chicken thighs.

Use tongs to put chicken in the pan.

Sear chicken thighs, 5 min on side one, season the opposite side and 3 min on side 2 .

Chicken will render a little fat, but you can add a little more oil if you want to

Remove and set aside chicken on a plate

Add 1/3 cup broth to deglaze the pan, scrape the bits with a wooden spoon (do not skip this step!). If there are any stuck-on spots, be sure and lift those away from the pan with a wooden spoon.

Add shallot, mushroom and carrots, and cook for 3 minutes.

Add garlic, and continue to cook for another minute.

Add remaining 1 and ½ cups of chicken stock, rice, thyme and stir together.

Place the chicken thighs on top of the mixture.

Place the lid on, and lock it, setting the valve to sealing.

Cook on manual high pressure for 10 minutes, and allow the Instant Pot to release naturally (do not use the quick release lever).

Switch the valve release, and remove the lid carefully.

Use two forks to shred the chicken, and stir the pot.

Serve immediately.

Whole Chicken

Total Time: 35 mins

Servings: 5

INGREDIENTS

2 tbsp. olive oil

1 1/2 c. chicken broth

3 medium red potatoes

1 whole chicken

Pinch of favorite spices

DIRECTIONS

Put your Instant Pot on Sauté low setting.

Add olive oil and put chicken inside to lightly cook for about 2 minutes, then flip chicken and cook on other side for 2 minutes.

Remove from IP and add your chicken broth and potatoes into your IP so they are close together so your chicken can sit right on top of them.

Place chicken on potatoes in your Instant Pot.

Close lid, make sure steam valve is secure, and set to poultry, normal setting, for 25 minutes.

When it beeps release steam valve.

When done releasing carefully lift lid and it is done!

Thai Peanut Chicken & Noodles

Total Time: 55 mins

Servings: 5

INGREDIENTS

1½ lb boneless skinless chicken breasts

1 c. Thai peanut sauce

¾ c. chicken broth

5 oz. stir-fry rice noodles

1 c. sugar snap or snow peas

optional garnishes - chopped peanuts, red pepper flakes, green onions & cilantro

DIRECTIONS

Turn your instant pot to Sauté and lightly Sauté the peas for 1-2 until just slightly cooked. Remove peas and set aside. Turn off of Sauté.

Add the chicken, Thai peanut sauce and broth to the pot. Cook on high pressure for 12 minutes.

Release the steam by turning the nozzle and remove the chicken from pot, leaving the sauce. To the sauce, add the noodles and ensure all of the dry noodles are submerged in sauce. Top with the peas and replace the cover as quickly as possible. Change the settings to Instant Pot (normal), and cook for 10 minutes or until the noodles are soft but firm.

Meanwhile, shred the chicken breasts and set aside.

Remove the lid of the Instant Pot and give the noodles a good stir. Add the chicken back to the pot with the noodles. Cook on Instant Pot mode for an additional 10 minutes. Serve warm.

Chinese Pork Tenderloin

Total Time: 20 mins

Servings: 1-2

INGREDIENTS

2 pounds of pork tenderloin

1 cup of beef broth, divided in half

1/4 cup of light brown sugar

2 tsp of kosher salt

1.5 tsp of Chinese Five Spice, divided into 1 tsp and 1/2 tsp

1/2 tsp of paprika

2 tbsp of soy sauce

1 tbsp of cooking sherry

1/4 cup + 1 tbsp of hoisin sauce, divided into 1/4 cup and 1 tbsp

1 tbsp of crushed garlic

1/2 tbsp of crushed ginger

1 tsp of white miso paste

1/3 cup of honey

2 tbsp of cornstarch + 2 tbsp of water to form a cornstarch slurry

DIRECTIONS

Take the pork tenderloin (usually two come in the pack) and slice it into medallions/discs about 1/2-inch thick. Place the pork medallions into a gallon freezer bag and set aside

In a mixing bowl, make the marinade by combining 1/2 cup of the beef broth, the brown sugar, kosher salt, 1 tsp of the Chinese Five Spice, paprika, soy sauce, cooking sherry, 1 tbsp of hoisin sauce, crushed garlic, crushed ginger and miso paste (if using). Mix together very well and then pour over the pork in the bag. Press the air out of the bag, seal tightly and place in the refrigerator for 24 hours, flipping once mid-way through.

24 hours later, dump the bag with the pork and all of its marinade into the Instant Pot. Add in the additional 1/2 cup of beef broth, 1/4 cup of hoisin sauce, 1/2 tsp of Chinese Five Spice and 1/3 cup of honey. Mix well and make sure the pork is nice and submerged into the marinade.

Secure the lid and cook on "Manual" or "Pressure Cook" High Pressure for 8 minutes. Allow a 10-minute natural release and follow with a quick release.

When done cooking, use a slotted spoon to transfer the pork to a serving dish. Then, take the sauce from the pot and carefully pour it through a strainer and into a bowl. Allow the strainer to catch all the excess fat from the pork, discard and return the strained sauce back to the Instant Pot

Hit "Keep Warm/Cancel" on the Instant Pot and then "Sauté" and adjust to the "High" or "More" setting. Add in the corn-starch slurry and stir well. Allow the sauce to bubble for a minute as this is what causes it to thicken up. After a minute of bubbling, turn the pot off and allow it to simmer down so it's only slightly bubbling. Give it a good stir. The sauce will begin to thicken.

Bbq Pulled Pork

Total Time: 1 hour 45 mins

Servings: 10-12

INGREDIENTS

2 tablespoons smoked paprika

1 tablespoon packed light brown sugar

2 teaspoons garlic powder

1 teaspoon freshly-ground black pepper

1 teaspoon ground mustard

1 teaspoon Kosher salt

3-4 pound boneless pork roast* cut into 2-inch cubes

1 tablespoon olive oil

2 cups of your favorite BBQ sauce, divided

1 cup chicken stock or water

DIRECTIONS

Whisk together the smoked paprika, brown sugar, garlic powder, black pepper, mustard and salt in a large bowl until evenly combined. Add the pork, then gently toss with the spice blend until it is evenly coated. Cover and refrigerate for at least 30 minutes, or overnight.

When you're ready to cook the pork, press "Sauté" on the Instant Pot. Add the oil. Then once it is hot (it will be shimmering), add a single layer of the pork pieces. Brown the pork on all sides, then transfer the pork to a clean plate and set aside. Repeat with the remaining pieces of pork. (This may take you 2 or 3 batches.)

Once all of the pork has been browned, turn the Instant Pot off. Then add the browned pork, chicken stock, and 1 cup of the BBQ sauce to the Instant Pot, and give the mixture a quick toss to combine everything. Twist on the lid, turn the vent to "Sealing", then set the Instant Pot to "Manual" for 60 minutes. Once the time is up, let the vent naturally release. (Don't do the quick release option.)

Carefully open the lid. Transfer the pork to a separate clean plate with a slotted spoon, leaving the juices behind. Press the "Sauté" button once more, and let the sauce simmer for 10 minutes or until it has thickened and reduced by more than half. Meanwhile, shred the pork with two forks.

Once the sauce has reduced a bit, skim some of the fat off of the top with a spoon or use a fat separator to separate and discard it. Then add the shredded pork back into the sauce, and give everything a good toss so that it can soak up those tasty juices.

Serve immediately, topped with an extra spoonful or two of the remaining BBQ sauce.

Kalua Pig

Total Time: 1 hour 60 mins

Servings: 8

INGREDIENTS

3 bacon slices

5-pound bone-in pork shoulder roast

5 peeled garlic cloves (optional)

1½ tablespoons Hawaiian Coarse Sea Salt

1 cup water

1 cabbage, cored, and cut into 6 wedges

DIRECTIONS

Drape three pieces of bacon on the bottom of your Instant Pot. Press the "Sauté" button and in about a minute, your bacon will start sizzling. (If you're using a stovetop pressure cooker instead, line it with three pieces of bacon, crank the burner to medium, and start frying your bacon.)

Slice the pork roast into three equal pieces. If you've got some garlic on hand, use it! With a sharp paring knife, stab a few slits in each piece of pork, and tuck in the garlic cloves.

Carefully measure out the amount of salt you use. For this recipe, follow Judy Rodger's rule of thumb: use ¾ teaspoon of medium-coarse salt for every 1 pound of meat. (Using fine salt. Use about half that amount.)

Sprinkle the salt evenly over the pork. As you're seasoning the pork, you'll hear the bacon sputtering in the Instant Pot. Don't forget to flip the slices, and turn off the heat when the bacon is browned on both sides.

Place the salted pork on top of the bacon, keeping the meat in a single layer.

Pour in the water. Check your Instant Pot manual to see what the minimum amount of liquid is for your particular model, and adjust accordingly. (After some digging and experimenting, I discovered that 1 cup of water is perfect for this recipe in my Instant Pot.)

Cover and lock the lid.

If you're using an Instant Pot, select the "Manual" button and press the "+" button until you hit 90 minutes under high pressure. Once the pot is programmed, walk away.

When the stew is finished cooking, the Instant Pot will switch automatically to its "Keep Warm" mode. If you're at home, press the "Keep Warm/Cancel" button to turn off the cooker and let the pressure come down naturally quicker.

Once the cooker is depressurized, check that the pork is fork-tender. If the meat's not yet fall-apart tender, you can always cook the pork under pressure for another 5-10 minutes to get the right texture.

Transfer the cooked pork to a large bowl, and taste the cooking liquid remaining in the pot. Adjust the seasoning with water or salt if needed.

Chop the cabbage head into six wedges and add them to the cooking liquid. Replace the lid and cook the cabbage under high pressure for 3-5 minutes. When the cabbage is done cooking, activate the quick release valve to release the pressure.

While the cabbage is cooking, shred the pork. Once the cabbage is cooked, pile it on the pork and serve.

Pork Chops, Rice and Vegetables

Total Time: 20 mins

Servings: 4

INGREDIENTS

1 tablespoon oil

1 cup onion, chopped

1 cup basmati rice, rinsed

1 tsp salt

1 tsp pepper

4 pork chops, thin cut

3/4 cup water

1/2 cup mixed vegetables, frozen

1 carrot julienned

DIRECTIONS

Place all ingredients into the inner liner of your Instant Pot in the order listed. Oil and onions at the bottom, rice with salt and pepper on top of that, pork chops on the rice, pour water and strew about the vegetables on top.

Cook at High Pressure for 5 minutes, and allow it to release pressure naturally for 10 minutes. Release any remaining pressure, and serve.

Honey Pork Chops

Total Time: 20 mins

Servings: 4

INGREDIENTS

2 pounds Pork Chops, Boneless

½ teaspoons Sea Salt

¼ teaspoons Black Pepper

¼ cups Honey

2 tablespoons Dijon Mustard

½ tablespoons Maple Syrup

½ teaspoons peel and mince Ginger, Fresh

½ teaspoons Cinnamon

¼ teaspoons Cloves, Ground

DIRECTIONS

Due to the nature of pressure cooking there is always room for inconsistency. The times given here are based on 4 servings fresh. If you are using more servings you may need to increase your cooking time.

Sprinkle pork chops with salt and pepper and place in the inner pot.

Set Instant Pot to sauté.

Brown pork chops on each side.

In a bowl, combine honey, Dijon mustard, maple syrup, ginger, cinnamon and cloves.

Pour over pork chops.

Lock cover into place and seal steam nozzle. Set on the manual setting for 15 minutes.

Naturally release pressure for 5 minutes and quick release remaining pressure.

Balsamic Pork Tenderloin

Total Time: 7 mins

Servings: 4

INGREDIENTS

2.5 lbs pork tenderloin

2 tbsp canola oil

1 cup chicken stock or canned low sodium chicken broth

0.5 cup Brown sugar

0.25 cup balsamic vinegar

2 cloves garlic, minced

1 tbsp Worcestershire sauce

1 tbsp grainy mustard

1 tsp ground sage

1 tsp Kosher salt

1 tsp freshly ground black pepper

1 tbsp corn starch

0.25 cup water to mix with corn starch

DIRECTIONS

Turn your Instant pot to sauté, and add canola oil. Once oil is heated through brown tenderloins.

Add remaining ingredients (except corn starch and water). Set on manual for 7 minutes.

Quick release the pressure when the timer rings. Check that pork tenderloin reaches 137F with a meat thermometer. Remove from pot and cover with aluminum foil to allow meat to rest.

Turn Instant Pot to sauté. Add corn starch to water and mix thoroughly. Add to Instant Pot and bring to a boil. Then turn off and on to maintain a simmer, until liquid has decreased by 50%. Taste for seasoning and add salt and pepper as needed.

Once the sauce is ready, cut the pork into medallions. Pour sauce over pork tenderloin and serve.

Boneless Pork Chops

Total Time: 10 mins

Servings: 5

Ingredients

1 tablespoon of coconut oil

4-6 boneless pork chops

1 stick of butter (or margarine)

1 package of ranch mix

1 cup of water

DIRECTIONS

Place the pork chops in the Instant pot with a tablespoon of coconut oil. Turn on the sauté setting and brown on both sides. Make sure all pork chops are browned. You can skip this step but they look prettier when you brown them first.

Place the butter on top and sprinkle the ranch mix packet on top.

Pour water (or chicken broth) over the pork.

Place the lid on and set to sealing.

Push the manual button and set to 5 minutes.

Allow it to naturally release pressure for 5 minutes and then do a quick release to remove the rest of the pressure.

Once cooked, serve.

You can even spoon the buttery sauce over the pork chops and over your veggies when serving.

Mexican Pulled Pork

Total Time: 32 mins

Servings: 1-2

INGREDIENTS

3-4 Lb. boneless pork roast, excess fat trimmed, cut into 2-inch chunks

1/3 cup taco seasoning

1 cup orange juice

½ cup chicken stock

¼ cup lime juice

DIRECTIONS

Season pork chunks on all sides with taco seasoning.

Add seasoned pork, orange juice, chicken stock and lime juice to the Instant Pot. Mix to combine. Cover.

Select "Meat" mode, then adjust until time reads 30 minutes, if necessary. Cook. When the time is over, turn off and let the Instant Pot release pressure naturally, about 10 minutes. Carefully turn the vent to release any extra pressure that might still be in there. Remove the lid.

Shred the pork with two forks.

To crisp up pulled pork: Preheat oven broil. Transfer it with a slotted spoon to a large baking sheet. Spoon 1/3 to 1/2 of the leftover cooking juices evenly on top of the pork. Broil for 4-5 minutes, or until the edges of the pork are brown and crispy.

Sprinkle with chopped fresh cilantro. Serve immediately or store for later use.

Maple Pork Stew

Total Time: 40 mins

Servings: 4

INGREDIENTS

2 lb pork shoulder or shoulder

1 tbsp olive oil

1 large onion

¼ cup maple syrup

1 orange

1 cup chicken/vegetable stock

A pinch red chilli flakes

9 oz baby carrots

2 celery sticks

10 dried dates

large handful fresh spinach

DIRECTIONS

Cut the pork into large 2-inch chunks.

Set IP to Sauté and when reads 'Hot' add the oil. Sear the pork until it has a nice golden crust.

Meanwhile finely chop the onion.

Add the chopped onion to the IP and stir well. Cook for 2 minutes until the onions are starting to soften.

Add in the maple syrup, stock, the juice of the orange and the chilli flakes.

Once the stock and syrup mixture are simmering cancelling Sauté and placing the lid on. Set the IP Manual for 25 minutes.

Whilst it is cooking prep your veg.

Wash and trim the baby carrots

Cut the celery into three chunks and then cut each chunk in half.

Chop each dried date into 3 pieces

Wash the spinach.

When the 20 minutes is up perform a Quick Pressure Release and add in the carrot, celery and dates.

Close the lid, press Manual and cook on high pressure for a further 5 minutes.

Do a QPR (quick pressure release), add in the spinach, salt to taste and serve.

Hawaiian Pork

Total Time: 85 mins

Servings: 4

INGREDIENTS

1 tablespoon oil

2 lbs pork roast

1/2 cup water

2 tablespoons Wright's Hickory Liquid Smoke

2 tablespoons soy sauce

2 tablespoons brown sugar

1/2 tablespoon Kosher salt

DIRECTIONS

Select Browning and add the oil to the cooking pot. When it's hot, brown the pork on both sides, about 3 minutes per side. Remove to a platter when browned.

Turn instant pot off and add the water, liquid smoke, soy sauce and brown sugar to the cooking pot. Add the pork and its juice juices to the pot. Sprinkle the salt over the top of the pork.

Select High Pressure and set timer for 60 minutes. When it beeps, use a natural pressure release to release the pressure, for about 20 minutes. When the valve drops, remove the lid carefully.

Remove the meat from the instant pot and shred with two forks. Serve immediately with some steamed rice.

Jamaican Pork Roast

Total Time: 45 mins

Servings: 12

INGREDIENTS

4 lb pork shoulder

1/4 cup Jamaican Jerk spice blend

1 Tbsp olive oil

1/2 cup beef stock or broth

DIRECTIONS

Rub the roast with olive oil and coat with Jamaican Jerk spice blend.

Set your Instant Pot to Sauté and brown the meat on all sides.

Add the beef broth.

Seal the top according to instructions and cook on Manual, high pressure, for 45 minutes.

Release pressure according to instructions, shred and serve.

Sweet Glazed Pork Loin

Total Time: 75 mins

Servings: 6-8

INGREDIENTS

Pork:

2 to 3 pounds boneless pork loin or pork sirloin roast, trimmed of fat

1 teaspoon ground sage or poultry seasoning

1/2 teaspoon coarse, kosher salt

1/2 teaspoon coarse black pepper

1 clove garlic, finely minced or crushed

1/2 cup water or chicken broth

Glaze:

1/2 cup brown sugar, light or dark

1 tablespoon cornstarch

1/4 cup balsamic vinegar

1/2 cup water

2 tablespoons soy sauce

DIRECTIONS

In a small bowl, combine the sage, salt, pepper and garlic. Rub the spices all over the roast.

Place the pork roast in the insert of the Instant Pot. Increase the water or broth to 1 cup and add to the Instant Pot. Secure the lid and cook on high pressure for 60 minutes (hit manual –> dial up or down to 60 minutes. Instant Pot will start automatically and count down the time). Let the pressure naturally release for 10 minutes before quickly releasing the rest of the pressure.

Near the end of cooking time (for either slow cooker or Instant Pot), whisk together all the ingredients for the glaze in a small saucepan and bring the mixture to a boil. Reduce the heat, and simmer, stirring occasionally, until the glaze thickens, 2-3 minutes. Season to taste with a pinch of salt and pepper, if needed/desired. Keep warm until ready to use.

Remove the pork from the slow cooker or Instant Pot. Shred the meat into pieces and place on a platter or plate. Drizzle the glaze over the pork and serve immediately.

Pork Tenderloin

Total Time: 50 mins

Servings: 4

INGREDIENTS

2 lb. pork tenderloin

1 cup hot water

Salt and pepper, to taste

1 Tbsp minced onion

1 tsp minced garlic

1 tsp dried oregano

1 tsp dried basil

1 tsp dried rosemary

Fresh veggies, as side dish

Dinner rolls, as side dish

DIRECTIONS

Place the pork roast into the electric Instant Pot insert with the hot water. Season with salt and pepper.

In a small bowl, toss together the minced onion, minced garlic, dried oregano, dried basil and dried rosemary. Add the herb mixture directly onto the pork roast, pressing lightly.

Steam valve: Sealing.

Cook on: Manual/High for 40 minutes.

Release: Natural or Quick.

Once finished cooking, slice the pork roast. Season with salt and pepper to taste.

Prepare veggies. Warm the dinner rolls.

Serve Instant Pot Herb Pork Tenderloin with veggies and dinner rolls.

Chile Pork Stew

Total Time: 1 hour 40 mins

Servings: 16

INGREDIENTS

4 lb pork loin Roast, cut into 6 pieces

3 - 7oz cans diced green chiles

3 poblanos, diced

1 red onion, diced (divided)

1 15oz can Rotel

2 Tbs chili powder

2 Tbs Goya Adobo Seasoning

1 Tbs paprika

¾ cup water

2 tsp salt - more to taste

Cilantro, lime and cotija cheese for garnish

DIRECTIONS

Cut the pork loin roast into 6 pieces and place in the Instant Pot along with 1 can of the diced green chiles (reserve the other two cans for after cooking), the diced poblanos, ½ of the diced onion, Rotel, chili powder, adobo seasoning, paprika, water and salt. Select 'manual' on the Instant Pot and set the timer for 50 minutes.

Once the time expires, allow it to naturally release pressure (approx 20 minutes)

Once the pressure is released, remove the lid and using the back of a spatula, start breaking up the pork pieces so that they become smaller shredded pieces. I personally like to keep some a little large, not completely smashing all of them.

Add the remaining two cans of diced green chiles and stir.

Serve with chopped cilantro, crumbled cotija and lime for garnish.

Pork Chops with Rice

Total Time: 20 mins

Servings: 4

INGREDIENTS

1 Tablespoon olive oil

4 bone-in pork chops

salt and pepper to taste

Dry ranch seasoning

2 cups chicken broth, divided

1 yellow onion, diced

3 carrots, diced

1 cup mushrooms, sliced

1 Tablespoon garlic, minced

1 1/2 cups uncooked Jasmine rice

2 teaspoons dried thyme (or 2 T fresh)

DIRECTIONS

Set Instant Pot to "Sauté" and add olive oil. While oil is heating, season both sides of pork chops with salt, pepper and homemade ranch seasoning.

Use tongs to put one or two pork chops in the pot and brown them on each side. Remove and brown remaining pork chops. Set aside on a plate once they are browned.

Add 1/2 cup chicken broth to the pot to deglaze the pot by scraping the stuck-on parts off the bottom of the pot using a wooden spoon. Make sure you get all the stuck-on parts lifted off or they will scorch.

Then add remaining 1 1/2 cups chicken broth, diced onion, diced carrots, mushrooms, garlic, uncooked Jasmine rice (rinse well first to wash away starch and prevent scorching) and thyme. Stir together and then place browned pork chops on top.

Place lid on Instant Pot and set valve to "Sealing". Set to cook on "Manual" for 10 minutes. Once finished, allow pressure to release naturally (for at least 10 minutes). Then remove lid and serve immediately.

Pork Tenderloin with Rosemary

Total Time: 20 mins

Servings: 6

INGREDIENTS

2.5 lbs pork tenderloin

1 cup bottled Balsamic Salad Dressing*

salt and pepper

2 tablespoons olive oil

1 cup broth, chicken or beef

For glaze:

2 cups orange juice

1 tablespoon fresh or bottled lemon juice

1/4 cup sugar

1 tablespoon + 1 teaspoon corn-starch

2-3 tablespoons fresh rosemary

DIRECTIONS

Marinate the pork in Balsamic dressing in a zip lock bag for 2-24 hours, turning bag over every few hours if possible.

When ready to cook, turn the Instant Pot to high sauté setting and remove the pork from the marinade, let excess marinade drain back into bag and set pork on paper towel. Discard marinade.

Add 2 tablespoon of olive oil to the Instant Pot.

Pat the meat to dry a bit with a paper towel and sprinkle generously on one side with salt and pepper.

Place the meat, seasoned side down in the hot Instant Pot.

Sear meat until browned on one side, before flipping the meat, season on opposite side with additional salt and pepper. Sear opposite side.

Using the manual setting, turn the pot to 25 minutes. Add 1 cup of broth (chicken or beef) to the Instant Pot.

Close and seal the lid into place.

When the timer goes off, allow the pot to naturally release pressure for about 15 minutes.

While the meat is cooking, pour orange juice, lemon juice, sugar and corn-starch into a small sauce pan and whisk until smooth.

Cook over medium high heat, bringing ingredients to a boil. Whisk and cook until the glaze is thickened, about 3-5 minutes. Add rosemary to sauce.

Remove from heat until ready to serve.

When meat is done, remove from Instant Pot and set on cutting board. Let sit for about 5 minutes before cutting. Slice into 3/4-inch slices with a sharp knife and place on serving platter.

Drizzle with some of the glaze, and place remaining glaze in a bowl and pass with meat.

Garnish with additional fresh rosemary leaves.

Pork Adobo

Total Time: 35 mins

Servings: 1-2

INGREDIENTS

3-4 lb. pork butt or shoulder cut into large cubes

1 cup soy sauce

1/3 cup apple cider vinegar

1-2 tbsp minced garlic

3-4 bay leaves

1 tsp black pepper

1 tsp oregano (optional)

Coconut oil or your preference

DIRECTIONS

Sauté pork with some oil for about 5 minutes.

Add remainder of ingredients and mix.

Cancel sauté and hit "meat"-adjust time to 25 minutes.

Be sure valve is at sealing.

Let Natural Pressure Release for 10 minutes, and then perform a Quick Release.

Serve over hot rice.

Peach Pork

Total Time: 90 mins

Servings: 1-2

INGREDIENTS

½ c orange juice

2 Tb soy sauce

3 cloves garlic, grated

2 Tb Sriracha sauce

1 Tb grated fresh ginger (or 1 tsp dry, ground ginger)

1 c peach preserves (jelly or jam)

2 lb pork tenderloin

Rolls for serving

DIRECTIONS

To begin, in a bowl combine the orange juice, soy sauce, garlic, Sriracha sauce, ginger and peach preserves. Whisk these together, breaking up the preserves as much as possible.

Place the pork tenderloin in your instant pot. You can cut it in half if you need to so that it will lay nicely in the bottom.

Pour the sauce over the top of the pork.

Place the cover on the Instant Pot, and press the "manual setting" on the controls and the set the time to 90 minutes. Allow your instant pot to cook the full cycle.

After it has cooked, pull the pork apart with two forks. Serve this on rolls.

Pork Chops with Apples

Total Time: 20 mins

Servings: 1-2

INGREDIENTS

4 bone-in ½" thick pork chops

Salt & pepper for seasoning

1 tablespoon olive oil

1 yellow, brown, or sweet onion, thinly sliced

1 teaspoon minced garlic

1 apple, cored and thinly sliced

1 teaspoon cinnamon

¼ cup chicken broth

DIRECTIONS

Season pork chops with salt and pepper, set aside.

Turn Instant Pot to Sauté setting, add olive oil and sauté onions in olive oil until soft, about 3-5 minutes. Add garlic, toss, and cook one more minute. Add apple slices and cinnamon, toss and sauté for an additional 2 minutes. Pour in chicken broth, season with salt and pepper, stir, and let sauté one more minute.

Add in pork chops, put on lid, and turn to Manual setting (on high pressure) for 3 minutes. Make sure valve seal on lid is in the "Sealed" position. After Manual cycle completes 3 minutes, let cook for 8 minutes, and then flip the valve seal so that the lid is flipped to "Release" to release remaining pressure. This will prevent the pork chops from overcooking.

Chops should be done through, or insert a meat thermometer to make sure it's 145-160 degrees. Serve immediately, topped with onion and apple mixture.

Teriyaki Pork Loin

Total Time: 1 hour 10 mins

Servings: 4

INGREDIENTS

1 small pork loin (2-3 pounds)

1 cup vegetable sauce

¼ cup soy sauce

½ cup water

2 tablespoons brown sugar

1 teaspoon ground ginger

1 teaspoon onion powder

2 cloves garlic, crushed

2 tablespoons honey

DIRECTIONS

In a small bowl, mix together all ingredients except vegetable stock and pork loin.

Pour vegetable stock into the bottom of the Instant Pot. Place pork loin directly into the pot. Cover with Teriyaki sauce.

Place lid on Instant Pot and set to seal. Cook on meat setting for 45 minutes for smaller pork loins or 1 hour for larger pork loins.

Allow to naturally release pressure.

Goan Pork Vindaloo

Total Time: 57 mins

Servings: 4-6

INGREDIENTS

For Spices

4-6 red chilis

1 bay leaf

1½ tsp cumin seeds

1½ tsp coriander seeds

1 two-inch piece cinnamon stick

6 cloves

10 peppercorns

1 tsp mustard seeds

For the rest:

2 lbs boneless pork loin chops, trimmed of excess fat, cut into one-inch pieces

2 large potatoes, peeled and diced

1 box chicken broth, 32 oz

1 large onion, diced

4 cloves garlic. chopped

1 one-inch piece ginger, chopped

1 tsp turmeric

1-2 tsp tamarind concentrate

¼ cup cider vinegar, or more to taste

salt and pepper to taste

DIRECTIONS

For the Spices

Heat a small pan on medium low. Add the spices and roast until fragrant, Let cool and grind.

For the rest

Press the Sauté button on the Instant Pot. When it says "hot" add the coconut oil. Add the onions, ginger, and garlic. Sauté until onions start to turn golden brown. Add the ground spices and the turmeric. Stir. Add the pork, chicken broth, tamarind, and vinegar. Stir. Turn the machine off, and then back on. Close the lid, and switch the steam release switch to closed.

Press the button for meat/stew and adjust the time down to 25 minutes.

Once it's done, release the steam. Open the lid and taste. Add salt and pepper to taste. Add the potatoes. Close the lid back and close the steam switch. Press the manual button, and adjust time to 7 minutes. Once done, release steam.

Serve hot with rice and naan.

Braised Pork with Potatoes

Total Time: 45 mins

Servings: 6

INGREDIENTS

2 1/2 pounds pork hock boneless, diced into 1-inch cubes and rinsed under cold water;

7 small potatoes, peeled and rinsed;

2 tablespoons olive oil

1 green onion cut into 2-inch long

2 teaspoons fresh ginger sliced

1 anise star

2 cloves

1 tablespoon anka sauce

1 teaspoon dark vinegar

1 1/2 teaspoons sugar

3 tablespoons light soy sauce

1 tbsp dark soy sauce

1/3 teaspoon salt

1 tablespoon olive oil

DIRECTIONS

Place the diced pork inside the Instant Pot and fill with boiling water.

Press "Sauté" function then "Adjust" button to set temperature to "More". Boil for 3 to 5 minutes, then rinse under cold water.

Clean and dry the inner pot. Select "Sauté" then set temperature to "More". Add 1 tablespoon olive oil and sauté the green onion, ginger, anise, and cloves for 1 minute.

Add anka sauce and sauté for another minute.

Put the cooked meat back into the Instant Pot, and sauté for 1-2 minutes.

Add the dark vinegar, soy sauces, sugar and salt to the Instant Pot and mix well.

Close the lid and place the pressure valve to "Seal" position. Press "Manual" and set to cook for 35 minutes.

While meat is cooking, quarter the potatoes into equal parts. Rinse under cold water, then pat dry with paper towel.

In a non-stick sauté pan on high heat, add 1 tablespoon of olive oil. Cook the potato pieces until golden brown.

When the Instant Pot program is done, allow for pressure to naturally release for 5 minutes. Quick release the remaining pressure then open the lid.

Remove cooked meat into a bowl and cover to keep warm.

Press "Sauté" button on "Normal" temperature. Cook the potato pieces with meat sauce for 7-8 minutes.

Place the cooked meat into the Instant Pot and gently stir for 1 minute.

Transfer to a serving bowl and serve immediately with rice.

Shrimp and Pork Dumplings

Total Time: 50 mins

Servings: 20-24

INGREDIENTS

1/2-pound tiger prawns finely chopped, or shrimps

1 teaspoon corn-starch

1/4 teaspoon salt

1/4-1/2 teaspoon oil optional

1/2-pound ground pork

2 tablespoons chicken stock unsalted

1 tablespoon corn-starch

1 tablespoon Shaoxing wine

2 teaspoons light soy sauce

1 teaspoon fish sauce

1 teaspoon sesame oil

1/2 teaspoon white pepper ground

1/2 teaspoon sugar

3/4 stalk green onions finely chopped

2 slices Ginger grated

1-2 shiitake mushrooms dried, re-hydrated and finely chopped (see tips)

20-24 wonton wrappers round

DIRECTIONS

Pat dry the shrimps with paper towels. Place the chopped shrimps in a medium mixing bowl. Add in 1 teaspoon of cornstarch and 1/4 teaspoon of salt.

Place the ground pork in a large mixing bowl. Pour in 1 tablespoon of corn-starch, white pepper, sugar, Shaoxing wine, soy sauce, fish sauce, sesame oil, and chicken stock.

Squeeze and mix the seasoned ground pork with your hands, then throw it against the mixing bowl until it resembles a paste-like consistency. Wash your hands and do the same with the seasoned shrimps. Put the pastes into the fridge and prepare the remaining ingredients.

Finely chop green onions and re-hydrated shiitake mushrooms. Grate the ginger slices.

Remove the pork and shrimp pastes from the fridge. Pour all the ingredients into the ground pork paste mixing bowl. Squeeze and mix the ingredients with your hands until blended. Remember to throw the paste against the mixing bowl!!

Place a wonton wrapper on one hand. Scoop roughly 3/4 - 1 tablespoon of mixed paste on the wonton wrapper with a butter knife or the dull end of a spoon. Then, wrap it into a cylinder shape with an open top.

Place a parchment liner into the bamboo steamer, then place the Shumai on the liner. Close the bamboo steamer lid.

Place a steamer rack and pour one cup of water into the Instant Pot. Place the bamboo steamer filled with Shumai into the Instant Pot. Close lid and cook on Manual at High Pressure for 3 minutes. Wait for another 5 minutes and do a Quick Release.

Pulled Pork with Cranberries

Total Time: 50 mins

Servings: 6

INGREDIENTS

1/4 cup spicy brown mustard

1/2 teaspoon garlic powder

1/2 cup coconut sugar or 1/2 teaspoon stevia

1/2 teaspoon Pink Himalayan salt or Celtic salt

1/4 teaspoon pepper freshly ground

3 1/2 pounds pork shoulder boneless, trimmed of excess fat

2 cups onions roughly chopped

1 cup cranberries fresh

3 cups cabbage finely shredded, for serving

1/2 cup pecans toasted and chopped, for serving

1/2 cup cranberries dried, for serving

DIRECTIONS

In a small bowl, combine mustard, garlic powder, coconut sugar/stevia, salt and pepper and mix well. Rub mixture on pork.

Add the pork to the Instant Pot and top with onions and cranberries.

Using the Manual function, adjust to high pressure and cook for 45 minutes.

When time is up, allow pressure to naturally release. Transfer pork to a platter or cutting board and shred with two forks.

Strain the liquid discarding the cranberries and onions. Pour the strained liquid over the pork.

Serve over shredded cabbage topped with chopped pecans and dried cranberries.

Keto Pork Meatball Bites

Total Time: 35 mins

Servings: 24

INGREDIENTS

1 1/4 pounds ground pork

2 strips bacon minced

1 egg mixed

1/2 medium onion minced

2 tablespoons almond flour

1 clove garlic minced

1/4 teaspoon pepper cracked

1/2 teaspoon sea salt

1 tablespoon tomato paste

1 tablespoon liquid aminos or tamari or soy sauce

2 tablespoons avocado oil or coconut oil

1 1/2 cups Water or chicken stock

2 tablespoons butter salted, melted

1/2 teaspoon xanthan gum optional

2/3 cup heavy cream 33%

1/2 teaspoon sea salt

1/4 teaspoon cracked pepper

DIRECTIONS

In a bowl mix the ground pork, bacon, egg, onion, almond flour, garlic, cracked pepper, sea salt and liquid aminos together.

Take 2 tablespoons of the meatball mixture and shape into a ball using wet hands. Place on a flat surface such as a cookie sheet.

Continue shaping meatballs. Makes about 24 weighing about 1 ounce each.

Press Sauté on the Instant Pot. Once display reads "hot", add avocado oil.

Carefully place half the meatballs into pot evenly spaced. After two minutes, turn them over.

After a minute, roll them onto a side. After another minute, remove and set aside on a plate.

Continue from step 5 to 7 with second batch of meat balls.

Once the second batch of meat balls are brown, remove and place with first batch.

Deglaze pot with water or chicken stock; be sure to scrape as much of the bits off the sides and bottom of the pan.

Add the meatballs back into the pot along with any drippings. Press cancel on the Instant Pot to stop Sauté.

Close lid and lock. Seal the pressure release valve. Press Manual and adjust to high pressure. Set time for 7 minutes to cook.

In the meantime, whisk xanthan gum into melted butter.

After cooking time is complete, press Cancel and Quick Release the pressure release valve. Unlock and open the lid. Remove the meatballs and set aside.

Press Sauté. Whisk in butter with xanthan gum into water/stock.

Next whisk in cream, salt and pepper in the Instant Pot. Let the sauce heat for 2 minutes while whisking.

Add the meatballs along with any drippings into the sauce and stir around to coat.

Ladle the meatballs with sauce into a bowl.

Beef Burgundy

Total Time: 40 mins

Servings: 1-2

INGREDIENTS

1 1/2 to 2 pounds beef chuck roast, cut into 1-inch cubes

salt & pepper

2-3 tablespoons gluten-free flour

2-3 tablespoons olive oil

1 small onion, chopped

3 cloves garlic, minced

3/4 cup red wine

1 tablespoon tomato paste

1/2 cup beef stock + 1 tablespoon gluten-free flour (whisked together)

1 teaspoon fresh thyme leaves

2 bay leaves

3-4 carrots, peeled and chopped

DIRECTIONS

Press the sauté key on the instant pot. Wait for the pot to say "HOT" before beginning cooking.

Spread the beef out in a single layer on a cutting board. Season the beef with salt and pepper. Sprinkle 2-3 tablespoons gluten-free flour over the beef and toss to evenly coat on all sides. Shake off the excess.

Add 2 tablespoons olive oil to the hot instant pot. Spread around then add the beef in a single layer (you may have to do this in 2 batches). Cook on one side until brown, about 4-5 minutes. Flip and cook on the other side for 2-3 minutes. (If the fond on the bottom of the pan starts to look like it's burning, add a little wine to deglaze so it doesn't burn - but ideally you want to wait to add the wine until everything is brown.)

Remove the beef from the instant pot and set aside. Add the onion (and another tablespoon of olive oil if needed) to the instant pot and cook until softened, about 3-4 minutes. Add the garlic and cook for 30 seconds.

Add the wine and scrape the bottom of the pan to remove the brown bits. Let cook for about 5 minutes until reduced.

Add the tomato paste and stir to combine. Add the remaining ingredients as well as 1/4 teaspoon salt and 1/4 teaspoon pepper.

Place the lid on the instant pot. Press the MEAT/STEW button and set the time to 40 minutes. After cooking is complete let sit for 10 minutes, then vent the pressure to open the pot.

Season to taste and serve. Enjoy!

Salisbury Steak and Gravy

Total Time: 45 mins

Servings: 6

INGREDIENTS

Steak:

1 1/2 lbs ground beef preferably grass-fed

3 TB whole milk I've used whole milk and cashew milk

1 TB Worcestershire sauce I like Annie's brand

1 garlic clove minced

1/3 cup panko breadcrumbs* unseasoned

1/2 tsp salt

1 tsp black pepper

1/2 tsp paprika I used smoked paprika

1 TB butter ghee or oil may work

Gravy:

8 ounces baby portobella mushrooms sliced

1 medium yellow onion thinly sliced

2 cups beef broth

1 TB tomato paste

1 TB dijon mustard

2 TB minced fresh parsley

1 tsp salt

1/2 tsp thyme

1/2 tsp black pepper

2-3 TB water

2-3 TB organic corn starch

DIRECTIONS

Add all the steak ingredients, except the butter, to a large mixing bowl. Combine the ingredients with your hands, being sure not to over-mix. Shape into 6 patties and set on a platter.

Let the steaks rest (for breadcrumbs to absorb moisture) while slicing the mushrooms and onion.

Whisk the gravy ingredients together, except the cornstarch and water, and set aside.

Set the Instant Pot to Sauté, Normal Temperature. Once hot, add the butter. Brown the steaks on both sides, in batches (about 2 minutes). Wash the platter, and return the steaks to the platter. Set aside.

Add the mushrooms and onions to the Instant Pot, and sauté lightly for two minutes. Add the gravy mixture to the pot, and scrape the bottom of the pot to loosen any bits (bits = flavor!).

Press the Cancel button and add the steaks on top of the mushrooms and onions. It's okay if they overlap in the pot.

Lock the lid on and set the Instant Pot to Manual High Pressure for 15 minutes. The valve on top should be set to Sealed. When the cooking time ends, let the pressure release naturally for 15 minutes. Then perform a quick release (turn the valve on the top to Venting) to be able to open the lid.

Remove the steaks to the serving platter.

Whisk the cornstarch into the cold water. Then add the mixture to the gravy in the Instant Pot, whisking to avoid lumps. Sauté the gravy until you reach the desired thickness (about 5 minutes for me). Pour the gravy over the steaks.

Serve the steak and gravy with mashed potatoes (recipe coming later this week) or egg noodles--Jovial makes great egg noodles. I've also been serving this meal with an easy side salad.

Beef and Broccoli

Total Time: 20 mins

Servings: 1-2

INGREDIENTS

1 & 1/2 lbs top round sirloin cut into strips

4 tablespoons soy sauce

4 tablespoons Chinese rice wine (Shaoxing style)

2 teaspoon corn starch

1/4 cup oyster sauce

1 cup beef broth

2 tablespoons brown sugar

1 teaspoon sesame oil

1 white onion finely chopped

3 cloves garlic, minced

1 tablespoon finely minced fresh ginger

olive oil

1 lbs. broccoli florets

DIRECTIONS

Marinate beef with 1 tablespoon soy sauce and 1 tablespoon wine for 1 hour in the fridge. Prep rest of ingredients while it marinates

Make beef & broccoli sauce. Combine 3 tablespoons soy sauce with cornstarch and mix until it dissolves. Then add 3 tablespoons of wine, oyster sauce, beef broth, brown sugar, and sesame oil and set aside.

Chop onion, ginger, and garlic and set aside.

Once the marinating is done, add oil to the Instant Pot on sauté and brown the beef. Remove beef and set aside.

Add more oil to the pot and sauté onion until translucent and then add garlic and ginger and sauté for about a minute.

Add beef & broccoli sauce and beef to the Instant Pot. Cook on high pressure for 12 minutes (Manual mode).

Once done, use the quick release pressure valve. Open the lid and add broccoli florets. Return pressure release valve to sealing mode. Select steam mode and reduce time to "0" minutes. Basically, the broccoli steams in the time it takes for the Instant Pot to heat back up to "steam" mode.

Once the steam mode is complete, do a quick pressure release again. Serve Beef & Broccoli over rice or noodles.

Korean Beef

Total Time: 20 mins

Servings: 1-2

INGREDIENTS

1 pound of lean ground beef (90% lean)

1 garlic cloves, minced

1/4 cup packed brown sugar

1/4 cup reduced-sodium soy sauce

2 teaspoons sesame oil

1/4 teaspoon ground ginger

1/4 teaspoon crushed red pepper flakes

1/4 teaspoon pepper

2-2/3 cups hot cooked brown rice

3 green onions, thinly sliced (optional)

DIRECTIONS

About 3-12 hours before you can season your meat up all but the green onions and oil.

In your Instant Pot turn on to Sauté and brown your meat for about 5 minutes with the oil. If you don't have sesame oil you don't have to go but you can use regular oil.

Now close the lid and cook for 5 minutes.

After done you will pour into a bowl and drain the fat.

Clean out your Instant Pot bowl really quick and place the rice in 3 cups water and 1.5 cups rice.

Shredded Beef

Total Time: 1 hr 30 mins

Servings: 4-5

INGREDIENTS

3 lb beef chuck roast

2 tablespoons olive oil

1 chipotle in adobo, chopped (seeds removed for less heat)

1 tablespoon adobo sauce (from the chipotle with adobo can)

2 teaspoons dried cumin

2 teaspoons dried oregano

2 teaspoons salt

1 teaspoon black pepper

½ teaspoon chili powder

1 cup lightly packed fresh cilantro, roughly chopped

1 onion, peeled and quartered

1 green bell pepper, seeded and cut into large chunks

1 cup water

DIRECTIONS

Salt and pepper the roast generously.

Press sauté on the Instant Pot and add the olive oil. Brown the roast on both sides, 3-4 minutes per side, or until completely browned.

If needed, remove the roast and drain any oil or fat. Place the roast back into the pot and spread the chipotle pepper and adobo sauce on top of the meat. Then sprinkle with the cumin, oregano, salt, pepper, and chili powder. Sprinkle the cilantro over the top. Add the onions and bell pepper. Pour the water around the edges of the roast in the pot.

Close the Instant Pot select high pressure for 60 minutes. When it's done and it beeps, turn the cooker off and use natural pressure to release. When the valve drops, remove the lid.

Remove the meat from the Instant Pot and let it rest for 5 minutes. Discard the veggies, reserving the liquid.

Shred the meat with 2 forks and return to the pot and stir into the liquid. Keep warm over low heat until ready to use.

Taco Meat

Total Time: 30 mins

Servings: 2

INGREDIENTS

2 pounds ground beef

4 tablespoons oil

2 red onions, diced

3 green bell peppers, diced

5 garlic cloves, minced

2 teaspoons chili powder

2 teaspoons oregano

1 teaspoon salt

1 teaspoon dried basil

½ teaspoon turmeric

½ teaspoon black pepper

1 teaspoon paprika

1 teaspoon cumin

½ teaspoon cayenne

½ teaspoon chipotle powder

Cilantro, garnish

DIRECTIONS

Add all of the ingredients to the Instant Pot except for the ground beef.

Press the "sauté" button and stir-fry for 5-6 minutes.

Then add the ground beef to the pot and cook until mostly brown.

Secure the lid, close the pressure valve and cook for 10 minutes at high pressure.

Once the meat is done, allow the pressure to release naturally (or you can quick release).

Open the lid, and if the meat released any liquid then press the sauté button to boil it off. This may take 10 minutes, depending on how much liquid the meat released.

Garnish with cilantro and serve.

Italian Beef

Total Time: 45 mins

Servings: 2

INGREDIENTS

3 lbs. beef chuck roast

3 lbs small red potatoes

3 cups carrots

¼ cup water

15 oz can tomato sauce

1 packet McCormick thick and zesty spaghetti sauce mix

DIRECTIONS

Quarter carrots and potatoes.

Layer potatoes at bottom of Instant Pot.

Layer carrots over potatoes.

Add water.

Layer beef chuck roast over carrots.

Mix tomato sauce and packet of McCormick thick and zesty spaghetti sauce mix. Pour over roast.

Cook on meat/stew setting for 45 minutes.

After 45 minutes, allow steam to naturally release before opening.

If you prefer a thicker gravy sauce, remove meat, potatoes, and carrots. Return roast to Instant Pot. Cook on meat/stew setting an additional 5 min. Serve.

Beef Bbq Recipe

Total Time: 1 hour 40 mins

Servings: 6-8

INGREDIENTS

3 lb. beef chuck roast

6 oz. can tomato paste

2 Tbs. yellow mustard

2 Tbs. dry minced onion

1 tsp. garlic powder

1 tsp. Real Salt

1 tsp. pepper

2 Tbs. apple cider vinegar

Water

DIRECTIONS

For added flavor, brown the roast first. (optional, will add 10-15 minutes to the recipe.) Press "Sauté" on the Instant Pot. When the display reads "Hot," add a Tbs. of cooking oil (coconut oil is a good choice) and let the roast sizzle a few minutes on each side. If you don't brown the roast, simply place it in the bottom of the IP.

In a 2-cup measuring cup, mix the tomato paste, mustard, onion, garlic powder, salt, pepper and ACV.

Add water to reach 2 cups total, stir, and pour over the roast.

Check the sealing ring and lock the Instant Pot, turning the valve to "sealing."

Press "Meat/Stew" and use the + or "Adjust" button to increase the timing to 60 minutes.

It will take about 15 minutes for the unit to get up to pressure and start the countdown timer.

When the cycle is finished and the IP beeps, allow 10-15 minutes for a natural pressure release (in other words, ignore it for a while). If you're in a real hurry, the meat will be cooked and just not quite as tender if you open the lid immediately after the cycle ends.

Open the valve to "venting" to release any remaining steam, twist off the lid, and use two forks to shred the beef. You can do this in the pot or on a separate plate. Sometimes it will be falling apart so much you just have to stir it up with a spoon and it shreds itself.

If you have the time, return the meat to the Instant Pot and put the lid back on for a bit while it's still on "warm" to allow the meat to soak up more juices.

Hamburger Helper

Total Time: 10 mins

Servings: 1-2

INGREDIENTS

1 pound of ground beef

2 cups beef broth

16 oz cheddar cheese

4 oz American cheese

1 tbs onion powder

1 tbs garlic powder

16 oz elbow macaroni

8 oz milk or heavy cream

DIRECTIONS

Sauté ground beef and seasonings until crumbled and meat is no longer pink.

Pour in beef broth uncooked pasta and milk. Place pot on manual high pressure for 4 minutes.

Perform a quick release and Stir in both cheeses. Serve.

Corned Beef and Cabbage

Total Time: 1 hour 30 mins

Servings: 12

INGREDIENTS

4 pounds corned beef brisket

6 cups water

2 tsp black peppercorns

4 cloves garlic

2 tsp dried mustard

1 head cabbage cut into wedges or 8 cups

2 onions or 1 cup sliced

4 carrots or 1 cup sliced into thirds

4 celery stalks or 1 cup chopped

DIRECTIONS

Place beef brisket into the pot. Discard the spic packet that comes with the meat.

Cover the beef with water; add more to cover if needed.

Add the spices into the pot.

Cover and set on "Meat/Stew" for 60 minutes on high.

Hit Cancel then use the Natural Release method, about 20 minutes.

Remove cover carefully, watch for steam, remove brisket and keep warm.

Add the vegetables to the pot and press "Soup" setting for 15 minutes.

Use the "Quick" Release method.

Uncover and add the beef back to the pot to warm through.

Smoked Brisket

Total Time: 90 mins

Servings: 1-2

INGREDIENTS

1.5 lb. beef brisket

2 tbsp. maple sugar, date sugar, or coconut sugar

2 tsp. smoked sea salt

1 tsp. black pepper

1 tsp. mustard powder

1 tsp. onion powder

½ tsp. smoked paprika

2 c. bone broth or stock of choice

1 tbsp. liquid smoke

3 fresh thyme sprigs

DIRECTIONS

Remove the brisket from the refrigerator about 30 minutes before cooking. Pat it dry with paper towels and set it aside.

Mix the spice blend by combining the maple sugar, smoked sea salt, pepper, mustard powder, onion powder, and smoked paprika. Coat the meat generously on all sides. The rub will get a bit sticky due to the sugar.

Set your Instant Pot to "Sauté" and allow it to heat up for 2-3 minutes. Grease the bottom with a bit of high heat cooking oil and add the brisket. Brown on all sides until deeply golden but not burnt. Turn the brisket to fatty side up and add the broth, liquid smoke, and thyme to the Instant Pot. Scrape the browned bits off the bottom and cover with the lid.

Switch the setting to "Manual" and increase the cook time to 50 minutes. Once finished, allow the Instant Pot to release steam on its own. Remove the brisket from the pot and cover it with foil to rest. Switch the Instant Pot to "Sauté" again to reduce & thicken the sauce (optional) with the lid off for about 10 minutes.

Slice the brisket on a bias and serve it with your favorite whipped and drizzle with the reduced sauce.

Mexican Shredded Beef

Total Time: 1 hour 95 mins

Servings: 8

INGREDIENTS

2 Tablespoons olive oil

3 Pounds beef chuck roast

1 teaspoon ground black pepper

1 teaspoon sea salt

3 Cloves fresh garlic (minced)

10 Ounce can diced tomatoes & green chilies

1/2 Large onion (sliced)

1/2 cup water

Juice of one lime (about 2 Tablespoons)

1/4 cup chopped cilantro

1 Tablespoon cumin

1 teaspoon chili powder

DIRECTIONS

Salt and pepper both sides of the chuck roast.

Select the Sauté button on your Instant Pot, and add the oil.

Brown the chuck roast on both sides, about 4 minutes per side.

Pour the tomatoes over the roast, and add the garlic and onion slices. Pour the water around the sides of the roast.

Place the lid on the Instant Pot, select the high-pressure setting, and set the timer for 75 minutes

The Instant Pot will beep when it is finished. Allow the built-up pressure to be released then remove the lid.

Shred the beef with two forks.

Remove the tomatoes and onions from the pot and return the shredded beef.

Add the lime juice, cumin, chili powder, and cilantro, stir to combine.

Place the lid back on top of the pot until ready to serve.

Instant Pot Beef Stroganoff

Total Time: 40 mins

Servings: 1-2

INGREDIENTS

3/4 cup flour

1 teaspoon salt

1/2 teaspoon pepper

1/4 teaspoon onion powder

1/4 teaspoon garlic powder

1/2 teaspoon dried thyme

1/2 teaspoon dried rosemary

1/4 teaspoon paprika

2.5 lbs. Sirloin Tip Roast, cubed

2-3 Tablespoons olive oil

2 cups fresh sliced mushrooms

1 medium onion, sliced

2-3 cloves garlic, minced

1 3/4 cups beef broth

3/4 cup sour cream

Cooked egg noodles, for serving

DIRECTIONS

In a gallon sized zip top bag, mix together the flour, salt, pepper, onion powder, garlic powder, thyme, rosemary and paprika. Add the cubed beef and toss to coat.

Set the Instant Pot to browning and add 2 tablespoons of oil. Working in small batches, taking care not to over crowd the pot, brown the meat on all sides. Remove the beef to a plate.

Add the mushrooms and onions to the Instant Pot, adding more oil if needed and cook for 5 minutes. Add the garlic and cook for an additional 1 minute.

Return the beef to the Instant Pot, along with any juices that have accumulated on the plate. Stir in the beef broth.

Place the lid on the Instant Pot and set it to high for 20 minutes.

After 20 minutes has elapsed, allow the Instant Pot to naturally release the steam. This will take 10-15 minutes. Carefully remove lid.

Place the sour cream into a small bowl and ladle about 1/4 cup of the hot liquid from the Instant Pot into the sour cream and stir.

Stir the sour cream mixture back into the Instant Pot with the meat. Season with additional salt and pepper, if needed, to taste. Serve over egg noodles.

Mediterranean Beef

Total Time: 50 mins

Servings: 1-2

INGREDIENTS

2 lb. boneless beef chuck shoulder roast, trimmed of any fat

3 tbsp. all-purpose flour

½ tsp salt

1 tsp black pepper

½ tsp dried oregano

1 large onion, finely chopped

4 shallots, sliced

2 tbsp. extra virgin olive oil

1 garlic clove, minced

½ cup beef broth

¼ cup red wine

¼ cup good quality balsamic vinegar

½ cup chopped, pitted Medjool dates

Optional: parsley or fresh oregano for garnish

DIRECTIONS

Whisk together flour, salt, pepper and dried oregano

Chop roast (slicing against the grain) into 2" size cubes

Place roast cubes inside a plastic bag and add flour mixture

Seal bag and shake to coat the meat

Turn Instant Pot on to "Sauté" mode and add olive oil

When the pot is hot, add beef mixture, onions, shallots and garlic

Sauté for 4-5 minutes until lightly browned, stirring occasionally to prevent burning

Add broth, wine, balsamic vinegar and dates and gently stir to mix

Put the lid on top and lock to seal

Press "Cancel" to stop sauté, then press "Manual" and set the timer for 40 minutes on high pressure setting

When cooking time has finished, use the "Natural Release" and allow the pressure to release on its own (takes about 15 minutes)

Serve over cauliflower rice, mashed potatoes, couscous or brown rice.

Beef Lo Mein

Total Time: 10 mins

Servings: 1-2

INGREDIENTS

1 16 oz. package of Pancit Canton Flour Stick Noodles

1 lb of flank steak, cut against the grain and into bit sized pieces

1 tbsp. of vegetable oil

1 tbsp. of sesame oil

1 bunch of scallions, chopped largely

1 tbsp of crushed garlic

½ tbsp of minced ginger

¼ cup of beef broth

1 tbsp. of Shaoxing wine

3 tbsp of low-sodium soy sauce

1 tbsp of oyster sauce

1 tbsp of red Chile paste

8oz of sliced mushrooms

A generous handful of snow peas

1 14oz bag of coleslaw mix

2 tbsp of pad Thai sauce

2 tbsp. of hoisin sauce

DIRECTIONS

Add the vegetable and sesame oil to the Instant Pot then hit "Sauté" and "Adjust" so it's on the "More" setting. Once the display reads "Hot", add the flank steak and stir for about 2 minutes until it's browned on all sides.

Add the garlic and ginger and stir for another minute

Add in the beef broth, Shaoxing wine, soy sauce, oyster sauce, red chili paste, scallions, mushrooms, snow peas and coleslaw mix. Stir up very well.

Secure the lid and hit "Manual" or "Pressure Cook" High Pressure for 4 minutes. When done, perform a quick release.

While our Instant Pot is cooking, take a large pot of water and bring to a boil on your stove.

Add the Pancit Canton noodles (probably in 2 batches as it's a lot of noodles) and cook for one minute. These are very delicate noodles and cook quickly. When done, strain.

Remove the lid from the Instant Pot and then add the noodles and then drizzle some additional sesame oil. Mix the noodles well with the meat, veggies and sauce in the pot and then transfer to a large serving bowl.

Once in the serving bowl, add in the pad Thai sauce and hoison sauce and tos..

Beef Vegetable Soup

Total Time: 8 mins

Servings: 6

INGREDIENTS

2 pounds ground beef or ground turkey

½ medium onion, diced

2 cups fresh or frozen Lima beans

2 cups frozen mixed vegetables

2 cups frozen corn

3 cans of diced tomatoes

2 cups water

Salt and pepper to taste

DIRECTIONS

Set your Instant pot to sauté setting. Cook meat and onions until brown and onions are soft.

Add all the other ingredients to the Instant pot.

Add lid and set to sealing.

Click the manual button and set the time for 4 minutes. Allow it to naturally release the pressure for 5 minutes and then do a quick release

Remove lid, stir, and add more salt and pepper to taste.

Serve hot with your favorite rolls and enjoy!

Ground Beef Shawarma Rice

Total Time: 20 mins

Servings: 8

INGREDIENTS

1 tablespoon vegetable oil

1 cup diced onion

5 cloves garlic

1 pound of ground beef

1.5 cups water or broth

1.5 cups basmati rice rinsed and drained

4 cups shredded cabbage

3 tablespoons shawarma spice

1 teaspoon salt

1/4 cup chopped cilantro for garnish (optional)

DIRECTIONS

Turn your Instant Pot onto Sauté on high. When the display reads HOT, add oil. When the oil is hot and shimmering, add the minced garlic and sauté for 30 seconds.

Add onions and ground beef. Stir while breaking up the ground beef clumps. Don't worry about cooking the beef at this stage, just break it up well.

Add rice, water, cabbage, salt, and shawarma spice

Cook on High Pressure for 5 minutes, and allow the pressure to release naturally for 10 minutes. Release remaining pressure.

Delicious Beef Bourguignon

Total Time: 30 mins

Servings: 7

INGREDIENTS

¼ cup (about 1.1 ounces) all-purpose flour

½ teaspoon salt

½ teaspoon freshly ground black pepper

1½ pounds boneless chuck roast, trimmed and cut into 1-inch cubes

2 bacon slices, diced

½ cup dry red wine

1 (10½-ounce) can beef broth

3 cups baby carrots (about ¾ pound)

2 cups sliced shiitake mushroom caps (about ½ pound)

2 teaspoons dried thyme

6 shallots, halved (about ½ pound)

4 garlic cloves, thinly sliced

7 cups hot cooked medium egg noodles

Thyme leaves (optional)

DIRECTIONS

Weigh or lightly spoon flour into a dry measuring cup; level with a knife. Combine flour, salt, and pepper in a large zip-top plastic bag. Add beef; seal and shake to coat.

Remove lid from a 6-quart Instant Pot. Press [Sauté], and use [Adjust] to select "More" mode. Place bacon in cooker, and cook, stirring constantly, 30 seconds. Add half of beef mixture to cooker; cook 5 minutes, browning on all sides. Remove beef and bacon from cooker. Repeat procedure with remaining beef mixture. Turn cooker off. Return cooked beef and bacon to cooker. Stir in wine and broth, scraping inner pot to loosen browned bits. Add carrots and next 4 ingredients (through garlic).

Close and lock the lid of the Instant Pot. Turn the steam release handle to "Sealing" position. Press [Manual]; select "High Pressure," and use [-] or [+] to choose 23 minutes pressure cooking time. When time is up, turn cooker off.

Open the cooker using Quick Pressure Release. Serve beef mixture over noodles. Garnish with thyme leaves, if desired.

Beef and Macaroni

Total Time: 30 mins

Servings: 1-2

INGREDIENTS

1 pound of ground beef

1 Tablespoon Olive Oil

½ Onion, diced well

½ Bell Pepper, diced (optional)

3 Garlic Cloves, minced fine

1 (25 ounce) jarred marinara sauce

1 (25 ounce) jar of water

1 (15 ounce) can Tomato Sauce

1 Tablespoon Worcestershire sauce

1 teaspoon Salt

¼ teaspoon Crushed Red Pepper Flakes

¼ teaspoon Ground Black Pepper

1 pound of rigatoni, or any other Macaroni

DIRECTIONS

Select Sauté or Browning on your Instant Pot and allow it to heat.

Add olive oil to the Instant Pot cooking pot and then dump in the beef and break into pieces as you brown. When meat is partially brown, add onions (and peppers, if using) and sauté until meat is mostly brown. Add garlic and sauté one more minute.

Drain excess grease, if needed.

Add the rest of the ingredients.

Lock on the lid and close the Pressure Valve.

Cook on High pressure for 6 minutes (or half the time indicated on your package of macaroni).

When Beep sounds, allow a 5-minute natural release, then put a paper or dish towel over the vent and do a quick release.

Top with freshly grated cheese.

Hearty Beef Stew

Total Time: 45 mins

Servings: 1-2

INGREDIENTS

2 lbs. Stewing Beef (cut into bite sized pieces)

1 Large Onion (finely chopped)

5-6 Cloves Garlic (finely chopped)

2-3 Cups Sliced Carrots or Baby Carrots

4-5 Medium Potatoes (cut into bite sized pieces)

1 Cup Frozen or Fresh Peas (optional)

1 Cup Frozen or Canned Corn (optional)

1-2 Pkgs Club House Slow Cookers Pot Roast or Beef Stew Mix

4-8 Cups Water

Olive Oil

Salt and Pepper to taste

Roux For Gravy

Butter

Flour

DIRECTIONS

Instant Pot Beef Stew

Turn your Instant Pot on sauté, add in some olive oil and wait for the display to say hot.

Once hot add in your onions and garlic, sauté for 2-3 minutes.

Next, add in your carrots and sauté for another 2 minutes.

In a large measuring cup mix 4 cups of water per 1 package of your Club House mix, 8 cups total water for a large batch in an 8 quart or 4 cups for a smaller batch or the 6 quart, and pour into your Instant Pot.

Next, add in your beef and potatoes, and then give everything a good stir.

Using the meat/stew button on your Instant Pot, set it for 35 minutes, ensuring your vent is set to the sealing position.

When the 35 minutes is up you will want to let your pot naturally release pressure for 15 minutes. The timer will start to count up, when it reaches 15 minutes you can proceed to quick release the remaining pressure and turn off/unplug your Instant Pot.

Add in your peas and corn, then give a good stir, they will cook as you make your roux to thicken the gravy.

Roux for Gravy

In a small pot on your stove on medium heat add in a chunk of butter and let it melt.

Once melted add in one spoonful of flour at a time, stirring until fully mixed each time. Do this until you get a semi-thick paste.

Add your roux into your stew and mix well until your stew thickens, then serve and enjoy!

Ground Beef Bulgogi

Total Time: 40 mins

Servings: 1-2

INGREDIENTS

2 tablespoons oil

6 cloves garlic, minced

2-inch knob ginger, minced

2 pounds ground beef

½ cup coconut sugar

2/3 cup coconut aminos

1 teaspoon crushed red pepper flakes

1 teaspoon salt

½ teaspoon black pepper

6 green onions, thinly sliced

2 tablespoons sesame oil

2 teaspoons sesame seeds

DIRECTIONS

Add the oil, garlic and ginger to the Instant Pot. Press the "Sauté" button and sauté for 2-3 minutes.

Add the ground beef to the pot and cook until mostly brown. Add the remaining ingredients to the pot and mix well.

Cover and lock the lid. Press the "Keep Warm/Cancel" button, and then press the ""Bean/Chili" button to begin pressure cooking. It will automatically be set for 30 minutes. Make sure the steam valve is closed. Once the meat is done, the Instant Pot will automatically switch to the "Keep Warm" mode. Allow the pressure to release naturally or use the quick release.

Open the pot and if the meat released a lot of liquid, press the "Sauté" button to boil off any extra liquid. This may take awhile, depending on how much liquid the meat released.

Stir the sesame oil and sesame seeds into the pot and serve.

Indian Beef Curry

Total Time: 60 mins

Servings: 6

INGREDIENTS

3 tablespoons vegetable oil for searing

2 pounds Beef Stew Meat cut in 1-inch pieces

salt for seasoning beef

black pepper for seasoning beef

1 cup onions chopped

5 teaspoons garlic minced

1 tablespoon Ginger chopped finely

1 jalapeno or Serrano pepper, or to taste, seeded and chopped finely

1 teaspoon black pepper freshly ground

1 teaspoon turmeric powder

2 teaspoons A-1 steak sauce

2 cups beef broth low sodium

1 1/2 cups carrots peeled, cut into 1-inch pieces

1 1/2 cups potatoes cut into 1-inch pieces

salt to taste

2 cups coconut milk canned, unsweetened

1/2 cup cilantro chopped

DIRECTIONS

Press 'Sauté'. Add oil to Instant Pot and working in batches, sear seasoned beef until browned on all sides, stirring frequently. Be careful not to burn.

Turn off Instant Pot if it gets too hot. Remove beef and set aside.

Turn Instant Pot off and add onions, garlic, ginger, jalapenos and stir well.

Press 'Sauté' again and add 2 tablespoons broth to deglaze Instant Pot, scraping up all the brown bits.

Sauté onion mixture till golden brown, stirring often. This will take about 5 minutes. If the mixture sticks to the bottom, add a tablespoon or two of broth.

Add reserved beef, black pepper, turmeric, A-1 steak sauce and sauté briefly to coat the beef with spices. Add broth and stir.

Close Instant Pot Lid, and make sure steam release handle is in the 'Sealing' position.

Cook on 'Manual' for 15 minutes (Make sure steam release handle is in the 'Sealing' position.) When time is up, do a Quick Release.

Add potatoes and carrots to Instant Pot. Cook on 'Manual' for 5 minutes (Make sure steam release handle is in the 'Sealing' position.)

Allow Instant Pot to release naturally for 10 minutes, and release any remaining pressure to open the Instant Pot.

Add coconut milk to the Instant Pot beef curry and stir to combine. Taste and season with salt to taste.

Press 'Sauté' and heat through.

Turn off Instant Pot, sprinkle beef curry with cilantro and serve with crusty bread or over rice.

Corned Beef and Cabbage

Total Time: 70 mins

Servings: 1-2

INGREDIENTS

Corned Beef

3-4 pound Corned Beef Brisket

3 cups Beef Broth

3 cups Water

Seasoning packet from corned beef

1/2 cup yellow onion, minced fine

3 Garlic Cloves, peeled and whole

15 whole peppercorns

The rest

6 Red Potatoes, rinsed and cut into bite sized pieces

5 Carrots, peeled and cut into 2-3 inch pieces

1/2 and onion, sliced

2 cloves Garlic, minced

½ teaspoon Salt

1 head green Cabbage, cut into 8 wedges

DIRECTIONS

Place corned beef in Instant Pot, fat side up

Add water, beef stock, seasonings, garlic, peppercorns, and onions.

Put lid on, and set to "sealed"

Use meat setting, or manual setting, and set to 60 minutes.

The display will turn to "ON" and after it is hot and pressure has increased it will start counting down.

When the time is up, wait for the pressure float to go down on its own, or vent it, and remove lid.

Remove corned beef from pot, place on a plate and cover with foil, set aside.

To the liquid in the pot, add the potatoes, carrots, onions, garlic, and salt, and put the cabbage on top of all of that.

Put lid on, set to sealed.

Press "Manual" and increase cooking time to 10 minutes on high pressure.

When finished, wait for pressure float to come down, or vent and remove lid.

Drain liquid off, and serve vegetables with sliced corned beef.

Beef Pasta Soup

Total Time: 20 mins

Servings: 4

INGREDIENTS

1 lb beef chuck, diced

1 yellow onion, diced

1 small can ground tomatoes

3 cups low sodium beef stock

1 teaspoon garlic powder

1 teaspoon Italian seasoning (basil, rosemary, thyme and oregano)

1 teaspoon paprika

1 teaspoon cumin

1/2 teaspoon crushed red pepper flakes

1/2 teaspoon salt

1/2 teaspoon fresh cracked pepper

10 uncooked lasagna sheets broken into pieces

Shredded mozzarella cheese, or Parmesan, for garnish

Fresh chopped parsley, for garnish

DIRECTIONS

Add diced beef, onion, ground tomato, garlic powder, paprika, cumin, Italian seasoning, chopped parsley, salt, pepper and red chili pepper flakes in the Instant Pot and mix well.

Add beef stock and broken lasagna, mix well to combine and cover with the lid.

Set to high pressure and cook for 20 minutes in soup/stew mode. After it is done, let the pressure naturally release.

Divide the beef and pasta into bowls or plates and garnish individual servings with desired amount of cheese and parsley. Enjoy!

Beef Spaghetti

Total Time: 10 mins

Servings: 1-2

INGREDIENTS

16 oz box spaghetti, pieces broken in half

1 lb ground beef

24 oz jar pasta sauce

1 tsp onion powder

garlic powder

2 cups water

shredded cheese for topping (optional)

DIRECTIONS

Set the Instant Pot to sauté and brown the ground beef, adding in the onion and garlic powder at the same time.

Remove the ground beef from the Instant Pot.

Add 2 cups of water to the Instant Pot.

Add the pasta to the Instant Pot.

Add the ground beef back into the Instant Pot.

Pour the sauce over top of the contents of the Instant Pot.

Set Instant Pot to cook on manual high pressure for 5 minutes.

Once the pasta is finished cooking, do a quick release of pressure.

Serve immediately, topping with some cheese if you like.

Stuffed Peppers

Total Time: 45 mins

Servings: 4

INGREDIENTS

1 Cup Water for the Instant Pot

For the Peppers

3/4 Cup Uncooked White Rice rinsed

4 Medium Bell Peppers any color

1 Pound Lean Ground Turkey or Beef

1 Egg beaten

2 tsp Garlic Powder

2 tsp Adobo Seasoning Powder optional

1 1/4 tsp Kosher Salt

1/2 tsp Ground Pepper

1 1/2 tsp Oregano dried

1 Tbsp Cumin Powder

1 Tbsp Chili Powder mild

1/4 tsp Chipotle Chili Powder hot

3 Tbsp Diced Green Chilis drained, 1/2 of a 7 oz can

1 Cup Tomato Sauce

DIRECTIONS

Rinse the rice well and add it to a large mixing bowl.

Rinse the peppers and cut the tops off. Deseed and remove the membrane.

Put the cup of water into the inner liner of the Instant Pot. Set Instant Pot to Sauté mode to begin heating up the water.

Add the ground turkey or beef (raw) and all other ingredients to the mixing bowl. Mix to combine thoroughly.

Fill each pepper with enough of the meat mixture to come a little bit above the top of the pepper.

Place stuffed peppers on a trivet in the Instant Pot. They will be sitting above the water.

Put the lid on and close it, turning the steam release knob to the Sealing position.

Cancel the Sauté mode off by pushing the Cancel/Keep Warm button. Then Press the Manual button, and the + or - button to select 15 minutes. Make sure High Pressure is selected. If not, press Cancel/Keep Warm again, press Manual, then the Adjust button to select High Pressure.

After the 15-minute cooking cycle ends, let the IP sit and it will enter the Natural Pressure Release phase, and let it count up to 10 minutes.

Manually release the remaining steam by turning the knob to the venting position (be careful! I use a wooden spoon to do this) When the pin drops and all of the remaining pressure is released, open the lid, facing it away from your face.

Check the internal temperature using an instant read thermometer. The temp should be at least 165 degrees for ground turkey, and 160 for ground beef.

Remove peppers with tongs to a plate and garnish with your favorite toppings.

Five Minute Cheesy Sauce

Total Time: 15 mins

Servings: 1-2

INGREDIENTS

2 cups peeled and chopped potato

1 cup chopped carrot

1/2 cup chopped onion

3 garlic cloves peeled and left whole

1/2 cup raw cashews

1/2 cup nutritional yeast

1 tablespoon chopped turmeric/ or 1 teaspoon turmeric powder

1 teaspoon salt

2 cups water

DIRECTIONS

Place all of the ingredients into your Instant Pot and lock the lid into place.

Make sure the nozzle on the lid is in the "sealing" position. Use the "manual" setting and set the timer for 5 minutes.

Use the quick release method when the timer is up.

Allow to cool for about 10 or 15 minutes and then transfer the mixture to your blender and blend until super creamy and smooth, about two full minutes.

Eggplant and Olive Spread

Total Time: 23 mins

Servings: 4-6

INGREDIENTS

4 tablespoons olive oil

2 pounds eggplant

3-4 garlic cloves, skin on (reserve one to use fresh at the end)

1 teaspoon salt

1 cup water or use

1 cup for electrics

1 lemon, juiced (about ¼ cup of juice)

1 tablespoons tahini

¼ cup black olives, pitted (reserve a few un-pitted for garnish)

a few sprigs of fresh thyme (about a tablespoon of leaves)

Fresh Extra Virgin Olive Oil

DIRECTIONS:

Peel the eggplant in alternating stripes of skin and no skin (to keep some of the flavor and color of the skin, but not too much!!)

Slice the biggest chunks possible to cover the bottom of your instant pot.

The rest can be roughly chopped. In the pre-heated instant pot, on medium heat without the lid, add the olive oil.

When the oil has heated, carefully place the large chunks of eggplant "face down" to fry and caramelize on one side, about 5 minutes - throw in the garlic cloves with the skin on. Then, flip over the eggplant add the remaining uncooked eggplant, salt and water.

Close and lock the lid of the instant pot.

Cook for 3 minutes at high pressure.

When time is up, open the cooker by releasing the pressure through the valve.

Take the instant pot base to the sink, and tip it to remove and discard most of the brown liquid.

Fish out the garlic cloves and remove their skin.

Add the Tahini, lemon juice, cooked and uncooked garlic cloves and black olives and puree everything together using an immersion blender (tilt the pan to get everything in the nook so it immerses the head immersion blender).

Pour out to the serving dish and sprinkle with fresh Thyme, remaining black olives and a dash of fresh olive oil before serving.

Crème Brûlée

Total Time: 30 mins

Servings: 6

INGREDIENTS

5 large egg yolks

2/3 cup plus 6 Tbsp. sugar, divided

1/2 vanilla bean, split lengthwise, or 1/2 tsp. pure vanilla extract

2 1/4 cups heavy cream

1/4 cup whole milk

DIRECTIONS

Insert the steam rack into the Instant Pot. Add 1 1/2 cups water.

In a large bowl, whisk together the egg yolks and 2/3 cup of the sugar. Scrape the seeds out of the vanilla bean and whisk into the egg mixture. Whisk in the cream and milk.

Pour the custard into six 4-ounce shallow ramekins. Cover each tightly with aluminum foil. Place on the rack, stacking them as necessary.

Lock the lid. Press [Manual] and cook on low pressure for 18 minutes. Use the "Quick Release" method to vent the steam, and then open the lid. Lift the ramekins out (they will be slightly wobbly in the middle). Let cool on a wire cooling rack for 25 minutes. Refrigerate, covered, for at least 4 hours, or overnight, until completely cool and set.

To serve, sprinkle the top of each custard with 1 Tbsp. of the sugar. Use a kitchen blowtorch or the oven broiler to caramelize the sugar until dark golden-brown. Serve immediately.

Banana Bread

Total Time: 25 mins

Servings: 6

INGREDIENTS

2 cups flour

1 1/2 cups sugar

1 stick of softened butter

3 ripe bananas mashed

2 eggs

2 tsp baking powder

1/2 tsp salt

1 tsp cinnamon

1 tsp nutmeg

6-inch spring form pan greased

DIRECTIONS

In a large bowl, mix together the eggs, sugar, and butter. Next add the baking powder, salt, cinnamon, and nutmeg.

Stir in the flour and bananas.

Grease your spring form pan and fill with the batter. Cover the top of the pan with a paper towel and aluminum foil. The towel and foil will prevent water from building up on top of the banana bread.

Next, place the trivet in the bottom of the Instant Pot and fill with 1 cup of water. Place the pan of banana bread on the sling and carefully use it to lower the pan into the Instant Pot.

Lock the lid into place and set the pressure valve to sealing. Using the manual setting cook on high pressure for 55 minutes. Let the pressure release naturally.

To remove the pan, use the sling to lift pan out of the Instant Pot. Remove the outer ring from the spring form pan, and let cool until ready to eat.

Sausage and Peppers

Total Time: 37 mins

Servings: 6

INGREDIENTS

1 package of Sweet Italian Sausage Links (Approximately 2 pounds or 14 links)

1 28 oz can of Crushed Italian Tomatoes

1 15 oz can of Tomato Sauce

1 Teaspoon Basil

1 Teaspoon Thyme

1 Teaspoon Oregano

½ Teaspoon Smoked Paprika

¼ Teaspoon Red Pepper Flakes

1 Teaspoon Sea Salt

½ Teaspoon Fresh Cracked Pepper

1 Teaspoon Minced Garlic

2 Tablespoons EVOO

1 Large Sweet onion (or 2 medium onions) sliced

3 Large Red Bells Peppers (cored and sliced)

DIRECTIONS

With your IP on Sauté, heat olive oil and add minced garlic. When the garlic becomes just a little golden in color, add your sausage links. Brown the sausage links on different sides to add color and release flavors. This should take about 5-7 minutes in total.

When your sausage is done, add in the onions, peppers, crushed tomatoes, tomato sauce, and all other ingredients on top. You do not need to stir.

Put the Instant Pot on Manual Mode for 26 minutes.

When the time is up, do a Quick Release

Release the lid and give it a nice stir to finish melding the flavors together.

Pumpkin Puree

Total Time: 15 mins

Servings: 1-2

INGREDIENTS

2 lb sugar pumpkin, halved with seeds scooped out

DIRECTIONS

Place 1/2 cup water in the bottom of the Instant Pot.

Place the pumpkin on the rack and cook high pressure 13 to 15 minutes.

Quick release and set aside to cool.

Scoop flesh out into a bowl and puree in blender or with an immersion blender.

Pumpkin Butter

Total Time: 5 mins

Servings: 1-2

INGREDIENTS

2 can of PURE pumpkin

1 cup of apple juice

4 tsp of pumpkin pie spice

1 tsp of ground ginger (optional, I use for joint support)

1/2 cup of sugar

DIRECTIONS

Simply place all the stuff in your Instant Pot and cook for 3 minutes on high pressure.

Once done it will be very hot and you will let cool for 3 hours.

Once cool place in the jars you have, use a marker and label them and place in the fridge.

Potato Salad

Total Time: 8 mins

Servings: 8

INGREDIENTS

6 medium russet potatoes, peeled and cubed

1 1/2 cups water

4 large eggs

1/4 cup finely chopped onion

1 cup mayonnaise

2 tablespoons finely chopped fresh parsley

1 tablespoon dill pickle juice

1 tablespoon mustard

Salt and pepper to taste

DIRECTIONS

Put the steamer basket in the instant pot. Add the water, potatoes, and the eggs. Lock lid in place, select High Pressure, 4 minutes cook time and press start.

When timer beeps, turn off instant pot and do a quick pressure release. When the pressure is released, carefully remove the lid. Remove the steamer basket from the pressure cooking pot. Put eggs into ice cold water to cool.

In a large bowl, combine the onion, mayo, parsley, pickle juice, and mustard. Add cooled potatoes and gently mix the mayonnaise mixture into the potatoes. Peel and dice three of the cooled eggs and stir into potato salad. Add salt and pepper to taste. If needed, add more mayonnaise to achieve desired consistency.

Chill at least one hour before serving. Top with slices of remaining hard-boiled egg.

Spaghetti Squash

Total Time: 10 mins

Servings: 2

INGREDIENTS

1 medium spaghetti squash (about 2 pounds)

1 cup water

DIRECTIONS

With a paring knife, cut the spaghetti squash in half, crosswise. Tip: You'll get longer strands of spaghetti squash if you cut it in half crosswise instead of lengthwise.

With a large spoon, scoop out the seeds in the center of the squash and discard the gunk.

Place the steamer insert/trivet into your instant pot. Add 1 cup of water to the pot.

Place the squash halves on the steamer insert. I put them cut-side up, but it doesn't really matter which way is up.

Place the lid on the instant pot and cook under high pressure for 7 minutes. On an Instant Pot, press the "Manual" button and hold the "—" button until the "30" on the display changes to "7." (If you're using a stove-top instant pot, you won't have to worry about pressing all those fancy buttons. Just cook on high heat until high pressure is reached. Then, reduce the heat to low to maintain high pressure for about 6 minutes.)

When the squash is finished cooking, release the valve at the top of the instant pot to rapidly lower the pressure.

Remove the lid from the pot and tip the squash halves to pour out the collected liquid. Check on the doneness by poking the squash with a fork. I like my spaghetti squash to be tender, but still toothsome—never squeaky. (If you like your squash more tender, cook under high pressure for an additional 1-3 minutes.)

Take the squash out of the pot and shred with a fork.

Sweet Brussels Sprouts

Total Time: 10 mins

Servings: 8

INGREDIENTS

2 pounds Brussels sprouts (1.5 pounds when trimmed)

1/4 cup freshly squeezed orange juice

1 teaspoon grated orange zest

1 tablespoon Earth Balance buttery spread

2 tablespoons maple syrup

1/4 teaspoon black pepper, or to taste

1/2 teaspoon salt, or to taste

DIRECTIONS

Trim 1/4 inch off the bottom of each Brussels sprout. If they are large, cut them in half. Otherwise, leave them whole. Rinse under cold water.

Place all of the ingredients in the Instant Pot.

Cover with the instant pot top, making sure that the quick release switch is closed.

Push the manual button and set it for 3 to 4 minutes if the Brussels sprouts are good size and whole and 2 to 3 minutes if they are very small or cut in half. If you like them harder than fork tender, you should set it for less time. You can always cook them longer if they aren't done to your liking by just setting the lid back over the pot and letting them sit in the pot a minute or two more.

When the time is up, hit the off button and quick release the pressure.

Stir until the Brussels sprouts are evenly covered with sauce and serve.

Roasted Potatoes

Total Time: 10 mins

Servings: 2-4

INGREDIENTS

1/4 cup avocado oil, olive oil, or ghee

1.5 pounds russet potatoes

1/2 teaspoon onion powder

1 teaspoon garlic powder

1 teaspoon (or more) sea salt

1/4 teaspoon paprika

1/4 teaspoon ground black pepper

1 cup chicken broth

DIRECTIONS

Slice the potatoes into wedges

Plug in your Instant Pot and press "Sauté"

Add in the cooking fat and allow it to heat up

Carefully add in the potatoes and cook them for 5-8 minutes, shifting them as they cook

Sprinkle the seasonings, pour in the broth and press the "Cancel/Off" button

Secure the lid, close off the pressure valve, and press the "Manual" button

Press the "-" button until your time display reads 7 minutes

Allow them to cook and then quick release the steam once completed

Let the steam exit completely and then remove the lid

Season with a bit of extra sea salt if needed

Butternut Squash Risotto

Total Time: 10 mins

Servings: 1-2

INGREDIENTS

A dab of oil for Sautéing the vegetables

1/2 a cup of chopped onion

3 cloves of minced garlic

1 red bell pepper, diced

2 cups of peeled and diced butternut squash

1 + 1/2 cups of arborio (risotto) rice

3 + 1/2 cups of vegetable broth

1/2 a cup dry white wine

1 package of white mushrooms (8 oz)

1 teaspoons salt

1 teaspoon black pepper

1/2 teaspoon coriander

1/4 teaspoon oregano

About 3 cups of greens - I used a spinach, kale and chard mixture

1 large handful of parsley

1 + 1/2 a tablespoon nutritional yeast

DIRECTIONS

Using the Sauté feature, heat the Instant Pot with a bit of oil

Add the onion, garlic, bell pepper and butternut squash and Sauté for about 3 - 5 minutes or until starting to brown

Add the rice, and stir well.

Add the vegetable broth, wine, mushrooms, salt, black pepper, coriander and oregano and stir well.

Close the lid and put the pressure valve to "sealed"

Click "manual" and reduce the time to 5 minutes

When Instant Pot finishes, carefully release the pressure immediately

Stir in greens, parsley and nutritional yeast and let sit for about 5 minutes to thicken

Serve warm

Store any leftovers in an airtight container, once cooled completely.

Macaroni And Cheese

Total Time: 25 mins

Servings: 8

INGREDIENTS

1 pound of pasta

1 teaspoon hot sauce

2 tablespoons butter

1 tablespoon dry mustard powder

4 cups water

1 cup of milk or half and half

1 pound of cheddar cheese

1 cup Monterey Jack cheese

DIRECTIONS

Place the following in the instant pot, the pasta, water, dry mustard, and hot sauce.

Pressure cook on high for 4 minutes. If the pasta needs to be drained, drain the pasta and place the pasta back into the pot.

Perform an instant release on the pasta.

Stir in butter, cheese, and milk and allow the cheese it to melt. Serve promptly.

Cabbage and Turkey Sausage

Total Time: 10 mins

Servings: 1-2

INGREDIENTS

1 lb Turkey Sausage (or other sausage), sliced

1 head cabbage cut/washed/sliced

1 onion (diced)

3 cloves minced garlic

2 teaspoons sugar

2 teaspoons balsamic vinegar

2 teaspoons Dijon mustard

olive oil

salt and pepper to taste

DIRECTIONS

In a large pot or in your Instant Pot, cook your sausage and onions in a bit of olive oil until slightly browned

Add your cabbage and the remainder of ingredients and Sauté until the cabbage cooks down quite a bit.

Taste the cabbage to check for seasoning, adjust with salt and pepper to taste.

Black Beans with Chorizo

Total Time: 1 hour

Servings: 6-8

INGREDIENTS

1 tablespoon vegetable oil

6 ounces Spanish-style chorizo, split in half lengthwise and cut into 1/4-inch half moons

1 pound of dried black beans

1 whole onion, split in half

6 whole garlic cloves

1 orange, split in half

2 bay leaves

2 quarts homemade or store-bought low-sodium chicken stock

2 teaspoons kosher salt, plus more for seasoning

Chopped fresh cilantro, for serving

DIRECTIONS

Heat oil in instant pot until shimmering. Add chorizo and cook, stirring, until it releases its fat and starts to crisp, about 2 minutes. Add beans, onion, garlic cloves, orange, bay leaves, chicken stock, and 2 teaspoons salt. Cover and cook at high pressure for 40 minutes.

For extra-tender and creamy beans, allow pressure to release naturally. For firmer beans, use quick-release valve on an instant pot, until pressure dissipates. Remove lid and discard onion, orange, and bay leaves. Season to taste with salt and serve. Sprinkle with fresh cilantro at the table.

Baked Beans

Total Time: 9 hours

Servings: 6-8

INGREDIENTS

2 cups dry Navy Beans

1 cup bacon, diced

½ medium onion, diced

1 tsp sea salt

1 tsp pepper

1 tsp dry mustard

1 tbsp Worcestershire sauce

1 tbsp balsamic vinegar

2 tbsp tomato paste

1/3 cup dark brown sugar

1/3 cup molasses

1 cup chicken stock

1 cup water

DIRECTIONS

Soak beans in cool water for at least 8 hours.

With the lid off of the Instant Pot, add bacon and turn on sauté function. Cook bacon for 2-3 minutes, until browned. Remove bacon to paper towel lined plate, leaving the fat of the bacon in the pot. Add onions and cook until soft. Turn off sauté function, and add in chicken stock stirring up the brown bits from the bacon with a wooden spoon. Mix in all remaining ingredients, then add in soaked navy beans. Liquid level should just cover the top of the beans, add more if needed. Leave out cooked bacon pieces.

Set the lid, selecting the bean function, increase time to 40 mins, and cook beans. Once cycle is finished, release lid and stir in bacon. Reseal the lid, and cook for an additional 10-20 minutes depending on liquid remaining.

Once final cycle is complete, set immediately or use keep warm function.

Spanish Rice

Total Time: 45 mins

Servings: 4-6

INGREDIENTS

1 tablespoon extra-virgin olive oil

1 tablespoon butter

1 cup white rice

Approximately 1 cup chicken broth or stock

Approximately 1 cup tomato sauce or puree

1 1/2 teaspoons chili powder

1 teaspoon cumin

1/2 teaspoon garlic salt

1/2 teaspoon dried oregano

1/4 cup diced fresh tomatoes, seeded & drained (optional)

DIRECTIONS

In a medium saucepan set over medium heat, melt together olive oil and butter. Add rice and stir to coat with oil/butter. Cook, stirring frequently, for about 2 to 3 minutes, until rice is toasted.

Stir in chicken broth, tomato sauce, chili powder, cumin, garlic salt, oregano, and diced tomatoes (if using). Increase heat to high and bring to a boil, stirring occasionally. Stir well, reduce heat to low, place lid on pot, and cook at a gentle simmer for 20 minutes.

If rice is not quite tender or liquid is not absorbed after 20 minutes, replace lid and cook for 2 to 4 minutes longer. Remove from heat, leave covered, and allow to rest for a few minutes. Fluff rice with a fork and serve.

Pico De Gallo

Total Time: 1 hour 15 mins

Servings: 4

INGREDIENTS

1.5 lb. tomatoes, roughly diced

1 red onion, finely diced

3 garlic cloves, minced

1.5 oz. fresh cilantro, finely chopped

1 Jalapeno, finely diced

Juice from 1 - 2 fresh lime

Kosher Salt

Ground black pepper to taste

DIRECTIONS

Prepare the Salsa Ingredients: Prepare the ingredients by cutting from driest to wettest.

Make Salsa Fresca: Add diced tomatoes, diced red onions, minced garlic, and chopped cilantro into a large mixing bowl. Mix well.

Taste one piece of finely diced Jalapeno to determine the spiciness level. Add in the amount of Jalapeno based on your personal preference (we added roughly 3 tbsp). Mix well.

Squeeze juice from 1 lime and mix well.

Season with Kosher salt & fresh ground black pepper. Mix well.

Taste and adjust accordingly. Make sure everything is balanced. Add in the juice from another lime if necessary.

Serve: Serve on top of tacos or as a side dish. It can be stored in the fridge for up to 3 days.

Calrose Rice

Total Time: 25 mins

Servings: 4

INGREDIENTS

1 cup medium grain Calrose rice

1 cup + 3 tablespoons cold water

DIRECTIONS

Optional Rinsing: Gently rinse rice under cold water. Drain well and reduce 3 tablespoons from the water.

Place 1 cup medium grain Calrose rice and 1 cup + 3 tablespoons cold water in Instant Pot. Close lid and pressure cook at High Pressure for 6 minutes (Please see experiment chart to find your preferred texture).

Turn off the heat and do a Full Natural Release (roughly 10 mins). Open the lid carefully.

Fluff & Serve: Fluff the rice with the rice spatula or fork, then serve with your favorite main dish.

Sticky Rice

Total Time: 27 mins

Servings: 2-4

INGREDIENTS

1 cup Glutinous Rice (No soaking required)

2/3 cup cold tap water

DIRECTIONS

Add 1 cup cold tap water and a steamer rack in your instant pot.

Add 1 cup glutinous rice in a stainless-steel bowl. Place the stainless-steel bowl on the steamer rack. Pour 2/3 cup cold tap water into the stainless-steel bowl. Ensure all the rice is submerged in the water.

Close the lid immediately and pressure cook at High Pressure for 12 minutes + Natural Release (roughly 5 – 7 minutes). Open the lid carefully.

Fluff & Serve: Remove stainless steel bowl from the instant pot. Gently fluff the sticky rice and serve warm with your main dish.

Coconut Rice

Total Time: 25 mins

Servings: 2-3

INGREDIENTS

1 cup Jasmine rice

Coconut Milk Mixture:

½ cup 100% pure unsweetened coconut milk or Thai unsweetened coconut milk

¾ cup homemade unsalted chicken stock

¼ - ½ teaspoon fine sea salt/table salt

DIRECTIONS

Rinse Rice: Rinse rice under cold tap water until clear. Drain well.

Create Coconut Milk Mixture: In a 2 cups glass measuring cup, mix ¼ - ½ tsp fine sea salt, ½ cup unsweetened coconut milk, and ¾ cup homemade unsalted chicken stock together. Mix well.

Pressure Cook Coconut Rice: Place 1 cup of Jasmine rice into the instant pot. Pour in all the coconut milk mixture and give it a quick stir to ensure all the rice is covered in liquid. Close lid and pressure cook at High Pressure for 5 minutes + 10 minutes Natural Release. The floating valve may drop at around 6 - 7 minutes, but don't open the lid until the full 10 minutes. Open the lid carefully.

Serve: Fluff the Instant Pot Coconut Rice and serve with your favorite main dish.

Congee with Minced Beef

Total Time: 1 hour 5 mins

Servings: 2-4

INGREDIENTS

2/3 pounds of ground beef

2.3 oz. spinach, roughly chopped

¾ cup Jasmine rice (using standard measure cup)

7 cups cold water

1 stalk green onion, finely chopped

Ground Beef Marinade

1/3 teaspoon fine sea salt

¼ teaspoon sesame oil

1/3 teaspoon ground white pepper

DIRECTIONS

Marinate the Ground Beef: In a mixing bowl, marinate 2/3 lb ground beef with 1/3 tsp fine sea salt, ¼ tsp sesame oil, and 1/3 tsp white pepper for 20 minutes.

Pressure Cook the Beef Congee: Add ¾ cup of Jasmine rice, marinated ground beef, and 7 cups cold water into the instant pot. Close the lid and cook at High Pressure for 25 minutes + Full Natural Release (~18 minutes). Open the lid carefully.

Thicken the Congee: The congee will look watery at this point. Add the roughly chopped spinach. Heat up the instant pot (Instant Pot: press Sauté button), stir until desired thickness & consistency. Season with salt.

Serve: Remove congee from heat and garnish with green onions. Serve with your favorite main dishes.

Cranberry Sauce

Total Time: 20 mins

Servings: 2-4

INGREDIENTS

12 ounces cranberries

2 ½ teaspoons orange zest

¼ cup freshly squeeze orange juice

Optional: 2 tablespoons maple syrup or honey

Pinch of salt

White Sugar, roughly ½ cup – 1 cup, - Use 40% - 70% of the total cranberries weight

DIRECTIONS

Wash the Cranberries: Remove the stems. Rinse cranberries under cold running water. Discard the soft, discolored & wrinkly ones.

Pressure Cook the Cranberries: Combine 2 tbsp. maple syrup and ¼ cup orange juice and pour into the instant pot. Add 2 ½ teaspoons orange zest and place 10oz cranberries into the instant pot. Reserve the other 2 oz. cranberries.

Close lid and pressure cook at High Pressure for 1 minute + 7 minutes Natural Release. Open lid carefully.

Make the Cranberry Sauce: Turn heat to medium (Instant Pot: Click cancel and Sauté button). Stir and break the cranberries with a wooden spoon. Add in the remaining cranberries and ½ cup of white sugar. Stir and the heat will instantly melt the sugar to form a thick cranberry sauce. Add a pinch of salt. Taste and add more sugar if desired.

Serve: Serve cold or warm with your favorite dish.

Basmati Rice

Total Time: 25 mins

Servings: 2

INGREDIENTS

1 cup Indian basmati rice

1 cup water

DIRECTIONS

Pressure Cook the Basmati Rice: Place 1 cup of basmati rice and 1 cup of water into the Instant Pot instant pot. Close lid and pressure cook at High Pressure for 6 minutes (Please see experiment chart to find your preferred texture). Turn off the heat and do a 10 minutes Natural Release. Release the remaining pressure (if any) and open the lid carefully.

Serve: Fluff the rice with the rice spatula or fork, and then serve with your favorite main dish

Chicken Tortellini Soup

Total Time: 10 mins

Servings: 8

INGREDIENTS

3 big boneless chicken breasts

1 small bag of carrots

3 stalks celery, chopped

2 medium onions, chopped

2 cloves garlic, minced

32oz chicken broth

2 tablespoons of butter

1 tablespoon Italian seasoning

1 teaspoon parsley

Salt & Pepper

2 packages fresh cheese tortellini

DIRECTIONS

Place all of the ingredients in the Instant Pot, except for the tortellini.

Cook on high pressure for 8 minutes.

Cook tortellini according to directions.

Quick release Instant Pot.

Remove the cooked chicken and shred.

Add chicken back to Instant Pot, stir well.

Add tortellini to Instant Pot.

Serve.

Smoky Mexican Chicken Soup

Total Time: 35 mins

Servings: 4

INGREDIENTS

1 Tbs. olive oil

1 onion, diced

1 green or red pepper, diced

2 c. carrots, chopped/diced/shredded (whatever is easiest for you)

2 cloves garlic, minced

3 chicken breasts or thighs

4 c. chicken stock

2 (14 oz) cans diced tomatoes (or one home-canned quart)

1 (7 oz) can tomato paste

2 tsp. chili powder

1 tsp. ground cumin

1 tsp. ground coriander

½ tsp. smoked paprika

½ tsp. salt

½ tsp. pepper

Fresh limes for juice

toppings: fresh cilantro, red or green onion, shredded cheese, avocado cubes, sour cream

DIRECTIONS

Turn the Instant Pot to "Sauté" and heat the oil.

Add the onion, peppers, and carrots and stir around for 5 minutes or so until they're starting to get translucent and fragrant.

Add the garlic for about a minute, just until you can really smell it, stirring constantly.

Add all remaining ingredients except for the limes.

Lock the lid in place and make sure the valve is closed.

Hit "Manual" on high and set it for 5 minutes (it will take about 10 minutes for the pressure to build and then the 5-minute-high pressure countdown will begin). If using frozen chicken breasts, add at least 10 minutes to the time.

When the timer goes off, allow the pressure to naturally release for at least 10 minutes before initiating a quick release (flip the lever on the lid from "seal" to "vent" - be careful of the steam!).

Check chicken for doneness (no pink!). It should be done, but if by chance it isn't, you can go for another 5 minutes on high pressure. It won't take as long to heat up, and then do a quick release and check again.

Remove the chicken from the pot and shred with two forks. Return to the pot and stir.

To serve, squeeze lime juice into each bowl or offer lime wedges at the table along with the optional toppings.

Chicken Enchilada Soup

Total Time: 50 mins

Servings: 5

INGREDIENTS

2 boneless skinless chicken breasts about 1 pound

3 cups chicken stock or broth

1 1/4 cup red enchilada sauce (recipe below) or 1 10-ounce can

1 can diced tomatoes 14-ounce, with juice

2 cans black beans 14-ounce, rinsed and drained

1 can whole-kernel corn drained 15-ounce

1 can diced green chiles 4-ounce

1/2 cup uncooked quinoa 93 grams

2 cloves garlic minced

1 medium white onion or 1 cup, peeled and diced

1 teaspoon ground cumin

1 teaspoon oregano

1 teaspoon sea salt or to taste

Optional toppings

chopped fresh cilantro diced avocado, diced red onion, shredded cheese, sour cream, tortilla strips/chips, squeeze of lime juice

Homemade Enchilada Sauce

1 tablespoons olive oil

1 tablespoons gluten free all-purpose flour can sub with arrowroot or tapioca starch for grain free version

2 tablespoons chili powder mild, medium, or hot

1/2 teaspoon garlic powder

1/4 teaspoon cumin

1/4 teaspoon oregano

1 teaspoon tomato paste

1 cup chicken or vegetable stock

salt to taste

DIRECTIONS

Soup

Add all of the ingredients to your instant pot and stir gently to combine. Lock on the lid, close the vent and use the manual settings to set the time for 25 minutes. After the 25 minutes are up, let the air vent naturally below opening the Instant Pot. After that you've opened the Instant Pot use a slotted spoon to remove the chicken. Transfer to a plate and shred before returning it back to the pot.

Serve still warm with your toppings and enjoy!

For the crockpot cook 3-4 hours on a high heat or 6-8 hours on a low heat. Remove the chicken from the pot and place on a chopping board. Use two forks to shred the chicken breasts and then return the chicken to the soup.

Serve warm and top with your garnishes of choice.

Homemade enchilada sauce

In a small sauce pot warm the olive oil. Add the flour and seasonings to the oil and stir together to form a roux.

Add the stock and whisk it all together to remove any lumps in the sauce. Let the sauce simmer on the stove for 7-10 minutes.

Remove from the heat until you're ready to add it to your soup or store it in an air tight container in the fridge. Use it within 3 days.

Beef Barley Soup

Total Time: 1 hr. 45 mins

Servings: 6-8

INGREDIENTS

1 ½ pounds stew meat

salt and pepper

2 tablespoons oil

10 baby bella mushrooms, quartered

3 cups mirepoix (a combination of chopped onion, celery, and carrots)

6-8 cloves garlic, minced

6 cups low sodium beef broth (or vegetable)

1 cup water

2 bay leaves

½ teaspoon dried thyme

1 large potato, shredded (using a food processor or grater)

2/3 cup pearl barley, rinsed

DIRECTIONS

Season the stew meat with a good pinch of salt and pepper. Heat 1 tablespoon of oil in a large pot or in the instant pot over medium high heat. Add ½ the stew meat and brown on all sides for about 2-3 minutes total. Remove meat to a plate and repeat with the second batch and the second tablespoon of oil.

Add the mushroom to the pot and brown the mushrooms for 1-2 minutes or until they start picking up the brown bits left behind by the meat. Remove the mushrooms to the same plate as the stew meat.

If needed, add a little more oil to the pot and the mirepoix mix. Cook the veggies for 4-5 minutes or until the onions soften and become translucent. Add the garlic and cook for an additional 30 seconds.

Add the stew meat, mushrooms, bay leaves, dried thyme, water, and beef broth to the sautéed veggies in the instant pot, cover and pressure cook the meat for 13-16 minutes depending on the size of the stew meat. Allow the pressure to release before removing the lid.

Add the shredded potatoes and the barley and allow the soup to cook on the high setting (for the instant pot you hit the slow cook button) for 1 hour or until the potatoes and barley cook through. Season with additional seasonings to taste. Serve warm with chopped parsley on top and a loaf of crusty bread or crackers.

Broccoli and Potato Soup

Total Time: 25 mins

Servings: 4-6

INGREDIENTS

2 tbsp butter

2 cloves garlic, crushed

1 medium sized broccoli head, broken into large florets

2 lbs Yukon Gold Potatoes, peeled and cut into small chunks

4 cups vegetable or chicken broth, plus more if needed

Salt and Pepper to taste

1 cup half and half

1 cup shredded cheddar cheese

6 slices of bacon (optional)

Chopped green onion or chives for garnish

DIRECTIONS

Select the sauté function on the Instant Pot.

Once hot, add butter and crushed garlic. Sauté about one minute, or until garlic begins to brown.

Add broccoli, potatoes, and broth. Season with extra salt and pepper. Secure the lid and select manual. Cook at high pressure for 5 minutes.

Once cooking is complete, select cancel and use the natural release for 10 minutes. Remove any remaining steam.

If using bacon, microwave or cook the bacon until desired crispiness. Set aside to cool.

Add the half and half and 1/2 cup of cheddar cheese. Blend with an immersion blender until smooth, or blend in batches in a large blender. If you want a thinner soup, add more broth. Add salt and pepper to taste.

Serve hot with remaining cheddar and bacon (if using).

Loaded Potato Soup

Total Time: 20 mins

Servings: 6

INGREDIENTS

8-9 Russet or Red-Skin Potatoes, skin on, diced

1 Carrot, diced

1/2 Onion, diced

2-3 cloves Garlic, diced

3 C. Organic Chicken Broth

3/4 C. Heavy Cream

4 oz Butter

Salt & Pepper, to taste

Optional: Garnish with shredded Cheese, Green Onions

DIRECTIONS

In your Instant Pot, add the potatoes, carrot, onion, garlic, broth and butter.

Put the lid on the Instant Pot, and set the pot to Manual (High) for 10 minutes & ensure the valve is closed completely.

Once the pot beeps, release the pressure, and use your Immersion Blender to blend half of the contents (you want half to be creamy and half to be chunky).

If you don't have an immersion blender, remove half of the pot and blend, then pour back in.

Add the heavy cream, and season with salt & pepper.

Garnish with green onions, shredded cheese and sour cream, if desired.

Chicken and Lentil Soup

Total Time: 45 mins

Servings: 8

INGREDIENTS

1 lb dried lentils

12 oz (3) boneless skinless chicken thighs, all fat trimmed

7 cups water

2 tbsp chicken Better than Bouillon

1 small onion, chopped

2 scallions, chopped

1/4 cup chopped cilantro

3 cloves garlic

1 medium ripe tomato, diced

1 tsp garlic powder

1 tsp cumin

1/4 tsp oregano

1/2 tsp Sazon or paprika

1/2 teaspoon kosher salt, plus more to taste

DIRECTIONS

Place all the ingredients into the instant pot, stir and cover. Use "Soup" button and cook 30 minutes. When done and the pressure releases, shred the chicken and stir.

Makes about 11 cups.

Carrot Ginger Soup

Total Time: 20 mins

Servings: 1-2

INGREDIENTS

1 cup chopped red onion 140g

5 cups chopped carrots 630g

3 garlic cloves chopped

2 tablespoons peeled and chopped ginger 30g

3 cups water 710ml

1 can coconut milk 13.5oz.

1 teaspoon salt

Black pepper to taste

DIRECTIONS

Prep the onion, carrot, garlic and ginger. The fastest way to do this is to use the "s" shaped blade of your food processor. This isn't totally necessary, but it makes it much faster. Place the prepped veggies into one big bowl and set aside for now.

Press the "sauté" button on your Instant Pot and let it heat up for about two minutes (make sure the lid is off).

Pour all the veggies into the Instant Pot and sauté for 5 minutes, stirring occasionally so nothing sticks to the bottom of the pan (make sure the lid is off). Turn the Instant Pot off.

Add the water and give it a stir. Lock the lid into place and make sure the nozzle is in the "sealing" position.

Use the "manual" setting and set the timer for 5 minutes. When the timer is up, turn off the Instant Pot and use the natural release method.

When the pressure is down, open the lid and add the coconut milk and the salt. Allow to cool for about 10 minutes, stirring frequently to help cool it down.

Use a blender stick or blend in batches with your blender until the soup is super creamy and smooth. Add a few turns of black pepper.

Tortilla Soup

Total Time: 45 mins

Servings: 4

INGREDIENTS

8 cups bone broth

1 tablespoon coconut oil

1 Pasilla Chile

1 onion

3 garlic cloves

1 28-ounce can of diced tomatoes

1 spring cilantro, plus more for garnish

1 teaspoon cumin

1 pound of chicken (boneless breasts or thighs)

Salt & pepper

Optional, for serving: avocado, cheddar cheese, corn tortillas (cut into strips and toasted), lime wedges

DIRECTIONS

Dice the onion and Pasilla Chile. Mince the garlic. Then, heat 1 tablespoon of coconut oil in the bottom of your Instant Pot on the sauté setting. Sauté the onion and garlic, for a few minutes, until the onion is translucent. Add the Pasilla Chile, and sauté for another minute.

Add the chicken to the pot, browning for 5 minutes on each side. Add the tomatoes, cilantro, cumin, a few dashes of salt, and a few cracks of pepper. Pour broth into pot.

Fit instant pot with lid, and set on Stew setting. Set timer to 20 minutes.

Once Instant Pot is done, release the pressure. Remove lid. Using a slotted spoon, pull chicken pieces from soup. Using two forks, shred chicken and then return to pot.

Serve soup in bowls and top with your favorite toppings.

Lasagna Soup

Total Time: 20 mins

Servings: 2-4

INGREDIENTS

2 tbsp. extra virgin olive oil

1 medium onion, chopped

½ green pepper, chopped

2 carrots, chopped

1 small summer squash or 1 medium zucchini, chopped

2 cups veggie ground round (or ground meat)

1 large can diced tomatoes -1/2 of the can blended, the other ½ left as is

4 cups vegetable stock

2 cups water

½ - ¾ box of lasagna noodles

½ tsp onion powder

1 tsp black pepper

1 tsp oregano

Sea salt, to taste

Optional: pepperoncini &/or chili flakes

DIRECTIONS

Turn on your Instant Pot and set to sauté. Place oil, onions, green pepper, and carrots in the Instant Pot. Allow to sauté 5-8 minutes, until the onions are translucent and just beginning to get golden brown. While this is sautéing, start breaking up your lasagna noodles into smaller pieces for use later. Add chopped summer squash and veggie ground round and sauté for 2-3 minutes. Add spices and stir. Add all diced tomatoes, broth, water, and lasagna noodles; turn the Instant Pot to manual (by pressing Cancel > Manual) and adjust the time to 4 minutes. At the end of the time, allow to depressurize naturally or do quick release after 5 minutes.

Optional: Serve with shredded cheese and/or sour cream on top.

Garden Harvest Soup

Total Time: 1 hr

Servings: 1-2

INGREDIENTS

6 cups of bone broth

10 cups of vegetables cut into one-inch chunks

One handful of fresh herbs

1 1/2 teaspoons sea salt

Freshly ground black pepper to taste

Chopped tomato or fresh herbs for garnishing if desired

DIRECTIONS

Place the broth and the chunked vegetables into the Instant Pot, making sure the soup is below the 4L mark.

Make sure your sealing ring is in place on the lid. Lock the lid onto the Instant Pot.

Place the steam release handle to the "sealing" position. It will not lock into place, but will remain loose. Just make sure it's pointing in the right direction.

Press the "soup" button. Press the "-" until you reach 15 minutes of cooking time. Within a few seconds, the Instant Pot will beep and display the word "on". This means that the cycle has started and the pressure is building. It can take a bit of time to reach full pressure - anywhere from 15-30 minutes. Once full pressure is reached, the display will switch to a countdown timer.

After the cycle is complete, the Instant Pot will beep again and the display will switch to L0:00. It's now in the keep warm setting. It will slowly depressurize in this setting. The timer will count up to 10 hours if left alone. Turn the machine off (by pressing the cancel button), let the Instant Pot naturally depressurize for 10-15 minutes, and then slowly release the pressure manually. To do this, put on an oven mitt, keep your face away from the steam release handle, and slowly turn the handle towards "venting". I do this in little bits, letting the steam escape before pressing the knob further. You will know when the pressure is fully released, because the float valve (the little sliver button next to the steam release handle) will fall down.

Once you have released the pressure, you can remove the lid.

Use a ladle to put the vegetables and the broth into a blender. You will probably need to do this in two batches. Puree the soup to your liking and then pour the soup into a large bowl. Repeat with the remaining vegetables and broth.

Season with the sea salt and pepper, adding more to your taste.

French Onion Soup

Total Time: 20 mins

Servings: 4

INGREDIENTS

4 large onions

3 Tablespoons butter

1 Tablespoon olive oil

5 cups vegetable stock

2 bay leaves

1 teaspoon dried thyme

1 teaspoon salt

1 teaspoon black pepper

4 thick slices French bread

4 slices Gruyere cheese

DIRECTIONS

Slice onions, taking care to cut them evenly, not too thick and not too thin.

Turn the Instant Pot to sauté.

Add butter and olive oil to the Instant Pot.

Add onions to the Instant Pot.

Sauté onions, stirring frequently.

Once onions are cooked and have turned brown, add vegetable stock to IP.

Scrape the fond from the bottom of the IP.

Add bay leaves, thyme, salt and pepper.

Attach the Instant Pot lid, set valve to pressurize.

Use the manual setting and set timer for 10 minutes.

Allow Instant Pot to do a NPR (natural pressure release), with the Instant Pot remaining on the keep warm cycle.

Turn oven broiler on.

Toast the French bread slices.

Spray oven-proof soup bowl with non-stick spray, add a slice of French bread toast to bottom.

Ladle soup, with plenty of onions on top of bread.

Add Gruyere cheese.

Broil until cheese is browned and melted.

Serve immediately.

Navy Bean Soup

Total Time: 20 mins

Servings: 8

INGREDIENTS

1-pound Navy Beans

2 Tablespoons Butter

1 medium Onion

3 cloves Garlic

3 Carrots

1/2 cup Celery

2 medium Potatoes

2 cups Chicken Broth

4 cups Water

1 cup Ham

1 teaspoon Salt

1/4 teaspoon Black Pepper

DIRECTIONS

Rinse and pick through the navy beans for any that are discolored, broken or floating in water. I just pour them into a colander and work from there.

Set the Instant Pot to sauté and put the butter in the bottom to melt.

After the butter has melted, add the onions and garlic and let simmer until translucent.

Add the carrots, and celery and sauté for about 2 more minutes.

Add the chicken stock and deglaze the bottom of the pot. Add the potatoes and beans.

Fill the pot with enough water to cover the beans and veggies and add the ham.

Sprinkle in the salt and pepper and give everything a good stir.

Click the cancel button and place the lid on the Instant Pot. Push the bean and chili button and wait for the countdown. Perform a natural pressure release when finished.

Minestrone Soup Recipe

Total Time: 18 mins

Servings: 4-6

INGREDIENTS

2 tbsp lard or olive oil

2 stalks celery, diced

1 large onion, diced

1 large carrot, diced

3 cloves garlic, minced

1 tsp dried oregano

1 tsp dried basil

Sea salt and pepper, to taste

28 oz can San Marzano tomatoes

15 oz can (or about 2 cups freshly cooked, drained) white or cannellini beans

4 cups bone broth or vegetable broth

1 bay leaf

1/2 cup fresh spinach or kale (without the rib) torn into shreds

1 cup gluten-free elbow pasta

1/3 cup finely grated parmesan cheese (omit for vegan option)

1-2 tbsp fresh pesto (optional)

DIRECTIONS

Set Instant Pot to sauté mode. Add olive oil, onion, carrot, celery and garlic. Mix until softened.

Add basil, oregano, salt and pepper.

If canned tomatoes are still whole, pulse tomatoes and liquid in can in a food processor or blender for a few seconds to dice tomatoes.

Add tomatoes, bone broth, spinach or kale, bay leaf, and pasta. Close lid and set to manual high pressure (HP) for 6 minutes. It will take about 8 minutes for the Instant Pot to reach high pressure, then it will cook for 6 minutes.

When timer goes off, let sit for 1-2 minutes. Then set to quick pressure release to vent steam.

Remove lid and add white kidney beans.

Serve in bowls and garnish with parmesan cheese and a dollop of pesto.

Chard Stem Soup

Total Time: 18 mins

Servings: 4-6

INGREDIENTS

8 Cups of Swiss Chard Stems diced

3 Leeks (green and white diced)

1 Celeriac peeled and diced

1 Potato peeled and diced

1.5 cups of Chicken Stock

1 cup of coconut milk

Salt and pepper to taste

DIRECTIONS

Add 2 tablespoons of oil to a pan or your Instant Pot. Cook the leeks until soft. (You can use the "sauté" function on the Instant Pot to cook your leeks.)

Add diced Swiss Chard, cooked leeks, celeriac, potato, chicken stock and coconut milk. (Note, if you want to can this recipe, you need to add the coconut milk when heating up the soup. I couldn't find any Ball recipes in which coconut milk was used as an ingredient and the final product could be canned.)

Add salt and pepper to the mixture.

Turn the Instant Pot to the "Soup" function and let it cook. Alternatively, put everything in a pot and bring to boil and simmer until the celeriac and potato are soft.

When cool, puree it with an immersion blender, or you can leave the soup chunky.

Enjoy.

Hearty Broccoli Soup

Total Time: 36 mins

Servings: 8-10

INGREDIENTS

1 Tbls. vegan margarine or vegetable oil

1 small white onion, diced

3 cloves garlic, diced

8 cups mushroom broth

1 C water

1 C Unsweetened Almond milk

2 large bunches of broccoli (4 heads), florets only

1 head of cauliflower, florets only

1 medium sized Japanese Yam or Yukon gold potato, peeled and cut into chunks

2 C prepared brown rice

1 pkg. Beyond Meat Lightly Seasoned Chicken Strips, thawed and diced

1 chicken flavored bouillon cube

2 Tbls. low sodium Tamari

½ tsp. salt

3 tsp. nutritional yeast (opt.)

1 tsp. Spike seasoning

dash of black pepper

DIRECTIONS

Add margarine to stainless steel insert, and press the sauté button. When margarine melts, add the diced onion. Sauté until softened, stirring occasionally.

Add garlic and sauté for another minute. Press Cancel on Pot to shut it off. Add broccoli and cauliflower florets, and yam/potato.

Add the tamari, salt, pepper, Spike, nutritional yeast, and bouillon cube. Pour the broth, milk, and water into the pot. Secure the lid and press Manual, and then press the (-) button to set the time for 6 minutes. Pot will say On.

It will take about 15 minutes to come up to temperature and build pressure. It will cook for 6 minutes and beep when done, at which point it will say LO and a number, which indicates how long the warming cycle has been going.

It will stay warm up to 10 hours or until you shut it off. Gently release the pressure by carefully and gradually opening the vent. Read the instructions and be careful not to burn yourself with steam. It is safe to open when the steam stops coming out of the vent and the stainless plug next to it lowers back into the starting position.

Open the pot, and use an immersion blender to puree the soup. When desired consistency is reached, stir in your cooked brown rice and vegan chicken. If they aren't already warm, wait about 10 minutes before serving.

Italian Soup

Total Time: 36 mins

Servings: 1-2

INGREDIENTS

1 3-4-pound whole chicken

1 cup large cut up carrots

1 head of escrole

1 28 oz can of diced tomatoes

32 oz chicken Broth

10 meat ball cut in quarters

2 celery stalks, chopped

1/2 pound of your favorite pasta

DIRECTIONS

Place your whole chicken in the instant pot with 2 cups of water. Set it on the poultry setting for 20 minutes.

Do a natural pressure release. Remove the Chicken all bones and remove all meat off the chicken.

The chicken will be falling off the bone. Place the meat in your Instant Pot.

Add in all your carrots, celery, full can of tomatoes, and chicken broth and your meatballs quartered.

The meatballs should not be bigger than 1" they will expand in the broth.

Place your Instant Pot on Soup setting for 10 minutes and use the Natural Pressure Release.

Remove lid and place your pot on sauté. Add in your pasta and Escarole.

Place on Soup setting for 2 more minutes and do a quick pressure release.

Mexican Chicken Soup

Total Time: 36 mins

Servings: 1-2

INGREDIENTS

3 boneless, skinless chicken breasts

2 teaspoons chili powder

2 teaspoons ground cumin

1 teaspoon salt

1 teaspoon pepper

1 28-oz can diced tomatoes

3 cups (24 oz) chicken broth

1 15-oz can black beans, drained and rinsed

1 10-oz can diced tomatoes with green chilis

1 4 oz can tomato paste

1 tablespoon of lime juice

DIRECTIONS

Place all ingredients except lime juice into Instant Pot.

If chicken is still frozen, set manual timer for 20 minutes.

If chicken was thawed, set it for 12 minutes.

Before serving, remove chicken from Instant Pot and chop or shred into bite size pieces.

Put chicken back into Instant Pot.

Stir in lime juice.

Top with your preferred toppings.

Beef, Beans and Tomato Soup

Total Time: 36 mins

Servings: 6

INGREDIENTS

1 tsp. olive oil

1 lb. lean ground beef

1 medium onion, chopped

1 T minced garlic

1 tsp. dried thyme

1 tsp. dried oregano

1/2 lb. fresh green beans, ends trimmed and cut into short pieces about 1 inch long)

2 cans (14.5 oz. each) petite-diced tomatoes with juice

2 cans (14 oz. each) beef broth

salt and fresh-ground black pepper to taste

freshly grated Parmesan for serving

DIRECTIONS

Turn the Instant Pot to sauté, add the oil and heat a minute or two, add ground beef and cook the beef until it's nicely browned, breaking apart with a turner as it cooks. When beef is browned, add the chopped onion, minced garlic, dried thyme, and dried oregano and cook about 3 minutes more.

Add the petite-dice tomatoes with juice and the beef broth and let them start to heat in the Instant Pot while you prep the beans. Trim beans on both ends, then cut them into short 1-inch pieces. Add beans to the Instant Pot.

Lock the lid closed and switch the Instant Pot to the soup function.

Season soup to taste with salt and fresh-ground black pepper. Serve hot, with freshly grated Parmesan to add at the table if desired.

Chunky Beef, Cabbage and Tomato Soup

Total Time: 30 mins

Servings: 7

INGREDIENTS

1 lb 90% lean ground beef

1-1/2 teaspoon kosher salt

1/2 cup diced onion

1/2 cup diced celery

1/2 cup diced carrot

28 oz can diced or crushed tomatoes

5 cups chopped green cabbage

4 cups beef stock

2 bay leaves

DIRECTIONS

Assuming your Instant Pot has a sauté option, or if using the Instant Pot, press the sauté button and let the Instant Pot get very hot, when hot spray with oil, add the ground beef and salt and cook until browned breaking the meat up into small pieces as it cooks, 3 to 4 minutes.

When browned, add the onion, celery and carrots and sauté 4 to 5 minutes.

Add the tomatoes, cabbage, beef stock and bay leaves; lock the lid cook high pressure 20 minutes.

Let the steam release naturally. Remove bay leaves and serve. Makes 11 cups.

Total Time: 35 mins

Servings: 1-2

INGREDIENTS

1 pound of lean ground beef

½ cup shredded carrots

2 cups cubed potatoes

16 oz can diced tomatoes

2 cups heavy cream

16 oz cheddar cheese

8 oz American cheese

½ small onion diced

DIRECTIONS

Place your Instant pot on sauté. Add ground beef and cook till brown and crumbled. Drain grease.

Add in chicken broth and veggies. Place pot on Manual High pressure for 30 minutes.

Do a quick release. Stir in heavy cream and cheese. Serve.

Cheesy Cauliflower Potato Soup

Total Time: 1 hr

Servings: 8

INGREDIENTS

1 pound of potatoes

1 medium head of cauliflower- cut away green leaves and chop head into several large chunks

1/2 lb bacon-chopped

4 cloves garlic-chopped fine

4 cups chicken broth

1 cup whole milk

1/2 tsp. pepper

1 1/2 cup grated cheddar cheese

DIRECTIONS

Set Instant pot to SAUTÉ. Press the + adjust button.

Prep and add in bacon and garlic. Cook about four minutes or until bacon is cooked to slightly browned.

Add in the peeled potatoes, chopped cauliflower and chicken stock. Place lid on and push vent to seal.

Press MANUAL button and Cook for 10 minutes on high pressure. Turn pot off.

Natural release for 10 minutes. Then quick release until pressure is totally released.

Remove the instant pot lid. Add in the milk and 1 1/4 Cup of the cheese. Mash the potatoes and cauliflower with a potato masher or immersion blender until you like the consistency. Add more broth as desired.

Serve with remaining cheese shreds and bacon crumbles on top as desired.

Creamy Thai Coconut Chicken Soup

Total Time: 15 mins

Servings: 4

INGREDIENTS

2 tablespoons oil

1 small onion, quartered

2 lbs skinless and boneless chicken breast or chicken thighs, cut into cubes

2 tablespoons Thai red curry paste (Mae Ploy brand)

1 red bell pepper, cut into strips

6 slices galangal, optional

6 kaffir lime leaves, torn and bruised, optional

3 cups chicken broth

2 tablespoons fish sauce or salt to taste

1 heaping tablespoon sugar

3/4 cup coconut milk

2 1/2 tablespoons lime juice

Cilantro leaves

DIRECTIONS

Turn on the Sauté mode on your Instant Pot. Add the onion and sauté for 10 seconds before adding the chicken. Sauté the chicken until the surface turns white.

Add the Thai curry paste, bell peppers, galangal and kaffir lime leaves (if using), stir to mix well. Add the chicken broth, fish sauce and sugar. Cover the pot and select High pressure for 10 minutes.

When it beeps, turn to Quick Release. When the valve drops, remove the lid carefully, add the coconut milk and lime juice to the soup, stir to mix well. Top with cilantro and serve immediately.

Tomato Basil Soup

Total Time: 15 mins

Servings: 2-4

INGREDIENTS

1 Small Onion, diced

1 T Olive Oil

1 Small Can Tomato Paste

3 15-ounce cans Diced Tomatoes

2 c Chicken Stock

2 teaspoons Parsley

1 Tablespoon Basil

1 teaspoon Garlic Salt

1 Tablespoon Balsamic Vinegar

1/4 Cup Sugar

DIRECTIONS

Turn your Instant Pot to sauté and let it heat.

Dice your onion.

Add olive oil, onion and tomato paste to the Instant Pot.

Stir and let cook for a few minutes until onion softens and turns translucent.

Turn off the Instant Pot and add your diced tomatoes (including the juices) and chicken stock.

Add garlic salt, basil, and parsley.

Turn the Instant Pot to soup, and set it for 10 minutes. Be sure the valve is set to closed.

When the timer goes off, let it sit. After 10 minutes, release the pressure and open the Instant Pot.

Stir in balsamic vinegar and sugar.

Use your immersion blender to puree.

Serve with Parmesan Cheese & a delicious Grilled Cheese Sandwich.

Sausage, Kale, And Sweet Potato Soup

Total Time: 30 mins

Servings: 6

INGREDIENTS

2 tbsp olive oil

1 lb ground turkey or pork sausage

1 medium white onion, chopped

3 cloves garlic, minced

2 large sweet potatoes, skinned and chopped

10 oz sliced mushrooms

5 cups chicken broth

1 cup dry white wine

2 tbsp apple cider vinegar

1 tbsp dried basil

1 tsp sea salt, plus extra to taste

½ tsp fresh ground pepper

3 cups roughly chopped kale

2 tbsp freshly chopped thyme (optional)

Get Ingredients Powered by Chicory

DIRECTIONS

Select the sauté function on your instant pot. Let it heat up (about 2 minutes). Add olive oil to coat the pot, and toss in ground sausage. Cook until almost cooked through, about 5 minutes. Add onion and garlic. Cook for another 3-4 minutes.

Add sweet potatoes, mushrooms, chicken broth, wine, vinegar, dried basil, salt, and pepper. Secure the lid.

Select manual and cook at high pressure for 8 minutes. Select cancel and use a quick release.

Open lid and add kale. Let cook with lid open for another 3-4 minutes, or until kale is softened but not wilted. Add additional salt if needed. Garnish with fresh thyme and serve.

Tomato Soup with Roasted Tomatoes

Total Time: 1 hr

Servings: 6-8

INGREDIENTS

Garlic Roasted Tomatoes:

3 lbs cherry tomatoes, halved lengthwise

14 whole cloves garlic, peeled and smashed

2 tablespoons olive oil

½ teaspoon salt

½ teaspoon black pepper

½ teaspoon red pepper flakes

Soup:

2 tablespoons olive oil

1 large onion, diced

1 red bell pepper, deseeded and diced

2 celery ribs, diced

3 tablespoons tomato paste

2 cups chicken or vegetable broth

1 teaspoon garlic powder

1 teaspoon onion powder

½ tablespoon dried basil leaves

½ teaspoon red pepper flakes

salt and pepper

1 cup heavy cream or half and half

Garnish:

½ cup grated parmesan cheese

fresh basil leaves

DIRECTIONS

Preheat oven to 425°F.

Place tomatoes and garlic on a baking tray, drizzle with 2 tablespoons of olive oil, season with salt, pepper and red pepper flakes, roast for about 25 minutes, or until soft and charred on the tops.

Remove tray from oven and set aside.

Set up the Instant Pot to the Sauté function and wait until it reads HOT.

Add 2 tablespoon of olive oil, once the oil heats up, about 30 seconds, add the diced onion, red bell pepper and celery ribs, season with the garlic powder, onion powder, dried basil, red pepper flakes, salt and pepper. Cook for 2-3 minutes, stirring occasionally.

Add the tomato paste and stir to combine. Add the garlic and roasted tomatoes with all the juices from roasting. Stir to combine.

Add the chicken or veggie broth, stir to combine. Adjust for salt and pepper and cover with the lid.

Select the Soup function, adjust temperature to MORE, adjust cooking time to 10 minutes.

Once the 10 minutes have passed, use a 10 Minute Natural Release (explained in the post) to release the pressure. After the 10-minute natural release, open the valve and release the remaining pressure. When valve drops carefully remove lid

Open the Instant Pot, Select the Sauté function, stir the soup, and stir in the heavy cream. Taste and adjust for salt and pepper. If the soup is too thick, you can add more chicken stock, ½ cup at a time.

Using an immersion blender or a Vitamix, puree the mixture until it's very smooth. I transferred the soup in two batches into the Vitamin to puree it, but if you use an immersion blender you can puree the soup directly in the Instant Pot.

Serve garnished with grated parmesan cheese and fresh basil leaves.

Ham White Bean Soup

Total Time: 30 mins

Servings: 8

INGREDIENTS

1 lb Great Northern beans soaked for 1 hour (see notes)

1 Tbsp olive oil

1 medium carrot chopped

1 medium onion chopped

3 cloves garlic minced

1 medium tomato peeled and chopped

1 lb ham cubed

4 cups vegetable stock

4 cup water

2 tsp salt

1 tsp freshly ground black pepper

1 tsp dried mint

1 tsp thyme

1 tsp paprika

DIRECTIONS

Press the "sauté" button on the Instant Pot, and add the oil, carrot, onion, garlic, tomato to the pot. Cook stirring occasionally for 5 minutes. (This is optional step. You can add everything in at once if you want).

Dump the remaining ingredients in the Instant Pot and close the lid. Lock the lid, move valve to sealing and cook on Manual for 15 minutes.

When the ham and bean soup is done, and you hear the beep sound, click the Cancel/Keep Warm button. Let natural pressure release for 10 minutes, and then quick release until all the pressure is out.

Open lid and serve warm.

Chicken Meatball Kale Soup

Total Time: 30 mins

Servings: 6

INGREDIENTS

For the meatballs

1 ½ lbs. ground chicken breast

2 tbsp. arrowroot powder or ¼ cup panko breadcrumbs

1 tsp. salt

1 tsp. pepper

½ tsp. crushed red pepper (optional)

1 tsp. garlic powder

1 tsp. onion powder

½ tbsp. dried oregano

½ tbsp. basil

2 tbsp. nutritional yeast or grated Parmesan cheese

For soup

6 cups low sodium vegetable stock

4 celery stalks, diced

2 medium onions, diced

3 medium carrots, peeled and diced

1 bunch kale, coarsely chopped

2 tsp. thyme

2 garlic cloves, minced

2 tsp. salt (or to taste)

½ tsp. crushed red pepper (or to taste)

2 tbsp. olive oil

2 eggs, beaten (optional)

DIRECTIONS

Make the soup base: On the HIGH SAUTÉE setting, add olive oil and heat for 1 minute. Add celery, onions, and carrots. Sauté for 3 minutes, until vegetables start to become soft. Add garlic, salt, thyme, and red pepper. Add in kale and stir to combine. Add vegetable stock and continue to cook.

Make the meatballs: combine all ingredients for the meatballs in a large bowl and mix well. Use a tablespoon to measure out meatballs. Wet hands to help create smooth balls and roll chicken mixture into meatballs. Continue to wet hands, if you feel the chicken sticking to your hands. Add chicken to the soup by gently dropping into the cooking soup. Do not stir or the meatballs will break apart.

Set the instant to high pressure: Cancel the sauté setting using the cancel/keep warm button. Set the Instant Pot to MANUAL PRESSURE and adjust pressure to HIGH. Secure lid on the pot and set to pressure for 15 minutes. Let the pot come to pressure. Once the cooker is finished, do a quick release and return the soup to the sauté setting.

Add eggs: Slowly drizzle in beaten eggs in a circular motion throughout the pot and cook for 2 minutes or until eggs are set. Turn Instant Pot off. Serve with grated parmesan if desired.

Broccoli & Bacon Soup

Total Time: 10 mins

Servings: 6

INGREDIENTS

4 rashers of smoked streaky bacon

1 tsp olive oil

1 large head or 2 small heads of broccoli

1 skinny leek roughly chopped and thoroughly washed

1 rib of celery roughly chopped

4 nuggets of frozen spinach leaves, or chopped

4 tbsp white basmati rice

Heel of a wedge of Parmesan cheese plus extra to shave over when serving

1 litre of vegetable stock

Lots of freshly cracked black pepper

Sea salt

DIRECTIONS

Start by setting your Instant Pot to Sauté and add the oil. Chop or cut the bacon with scissors into small lardons then cook until the fat has rendered out and the bacon is crisp. Stir constantly to prevent sticking. When cooked, remove the bacon with a slotted spoon to a plate until ready to serve.

If there is a lot of fat, pour most of it away then add all the vegetables and rice then stir very well to distribute everything then cover with stock and tuck the Parmesan rind in.

Cancel Sauté mode then pop the lid on, set to Manual for 5 minutes on high pressure.

When cooked, remove lid, retrieve the rind of the Parmesan, scraping any melted cheese into the pot then use a stick blender to purée your soup.

Taste for seasoning - add lots of black pepper but remember the cheese and bacon add salt so you will likely need a very small amount.

Serve ladled into bowls and garnished with a few small shavings of Parmesan and a few crisp pieces of the cooked bacon. Makes 6 large servings suitable for to serve as a meal with bread on the side to dunk.

Potato Soup with Cheddar And Leek

Total Time: 25 mins

Servings: 8

INGREDIENTS

2 tbsp unsalted butter

3 leeks cleaned and thinly sliced, white and light green

1 tsp kosher salt

4 cloves garlic crushed

4 sprigs fresh thyme

1 1/2 tsp dried oregano

2 leaves bay

3/4 cup white wine

5 cups vegetable broth make your own

4 medium gold potatoes peeled and diced

1 1/2 cups cream or half and half

1/3 cup grated cheddar cheese

DIRECTIONS

Using the sauté function, melt the butter in the instant pot. Once melted, add the sliced leeks and salt and sauté until soft. Add the crushed garlic; sauté for 30 seconds and turn off the sauté function

Remove a small portion of the leeks and set aside for serving

To the leek mixture in the pot add in the thyme, oregano, bay leaves, white wine, broth, and potatoes. Give it all a good stir and set to high pressure for 10 minutes

Once complete, quick release and open the pot. Add in the cream and use a stick immersion blender to puree the soup until it reaches the consistency of your liking

Set the instant pot to warm and heat the soup through.

Once hot serve up with a sprinkle of extra sautéed leeks, some crispy bacon and a sprinkle of cheese.

Beef and Beer Stew

Total Time: 50 mins

Servings: 1-2

INGREDIENTS

2 lb Beef Stew Meat, cut into bite sized pieces

1/4 Cup flour

1 Tsp salt

1 Tsp ground pepper

2 Tbsp Butter

1 Packet dry onion soup mix

2 cups beef stock

1 12oz bottle of beer (I prefer a larger but you could use whatever you like)

1 Tbsp minced garlic

1 Tbsp tomato paste

1 Tbsp Worcestershire sauce

2 cups uncooked medium egg noodles

Frozen peas and carrots, thawed (optional)

DIRECTIONS

Add beef stew meat, flour, salt & pepper to a large ziploc bag. Toss until evenly coated.

Turn Instant Pot on to sauté and add butter. When butter is melted add beef and garlic to pot. Brown meat on each side (about 3-5 minutes).

When meat is browned, remove with a slotted spoon and set aside.

Deglaze the bottom of the put with two cups of beef stock. When the bottom is clean, add the meat back in.

Add beer, tomato paste, Worcestershire, and dry onion soup mix.

Close Instant Pot and set to 35 minutes on manual high pressure.

When time is up, allow for a 10-minute natural release.

Once released add uncooked egg noodles and close top. Set for 1 minute on manual high pressure. Quick release when the time is done.

Stir in frozen veggies and allow sitting for around 5 mins (until warmed).

Andouille Sausage Stew

Total Time: 30 mins

Servings: 1-2

INGREDIENTS

1 pound of uncooked Pork Andouille Sausage, crumbled

1 medium sweet onion, halved and thinly sliced

½ pound grape or cherry tomatoes

1 1/2 pounds Yukon Gold potatoes, peeled and cut into 1" pieces

¾ pound collard greens, stems removed and thinly sliced

1 cup chicken broth

1 teaspoon kosher salt

20 to 25 turns freshly ground black pepper

1/2 medium lemon, freshly squeezed

DIRECTIONS

Peel and halve onion and thinly slice.

Peel potatoes and cut into 1" chunks.

Clean collard greens, remove ribs and thinly slice.

Set Instant Pot to Sauté. Add crumbled Andouille sausage and sauté for 5 to 8 minutes, stirring occasionally.

Add sliced onions and tomatoes. Mix and continue to sauté for an additional 3 to 4 minutes.

Add potatoes, collard greens and broth along with salt and pepper. Cover and set to Manual, High Pressure for 10 minutes.

Finish by adding fresh lemon juice. Adjust salt and pepper if necessary.

Vegan Hoppin' John

Total Time: 50 mins

Servings: 4-6

INGREDIENTS

1 small onion, chopped

4 stalks of celery, chopped

4 cloves fresh garlic, minced

1 stalk rosemary, tough stem removed, finely chopped

½ pound dried black-eyed peas

½ cup uncooked wild rice, rinsed

1 15-ounce can low- or no-sodium diced tomatoes

1 15-ounce can low- or no-sodium fire roasted tomatoes

2 cups chopped kale (I used curly and measured after I chopped it)

4 cups no- or low-sodium vegetable broth

1-3 cups water (to fill pot to halfway and make sure the beans are covered with liquid)

½ cup nutritional yeast

¼ cup no- or low-sodium vegetable soup base

DIRECTIONS

Using sauté function (High), add onion and celery to instant pot and sauté until just becoming translucent. Add the garlic and rosemary and stir for 1-2 minutes, make sure it doesn't burn. Hit Cancel/Keep Warm.

Add the rest of the ingredients to the pot, filling until halfway full with ingredients covered with liquid (use water to adjust level, but take care not to overfill). Close the lid. Use the Beans/Chili function and set timer to 25 minutes. Use Natural Release.

Vegan Green Chile Stew

Total Time: 1 hr 8 mins

Servings: 10-12

INGREDIENTS

Meat

1/2 package of Butler Soy Curls rehydrated

(Can also sub Seitan 1 tube GimmeLean Sausage, or 16oz Portabello Mushrooms

1 tsp Chili Powder

1 tsp Ground Cumin

1 tsp Garlic Powder

1 tsp Onion Powder

The broth

1 Yellow Onion diced

2 Carrots diced

2 Stalks Celery diced

4-5 Cloves Garlic

2 Cups Vegetable Broth

2 Cups Water

1 tsp Oregano

1 cup dried rinsed, Pinto Beans

The stew

3 Yukon Gold Potatoes cubed

15 oz Can Fire Roasted Tomatoes

24 oz package Select New Mexico Green Chiles

1/4 cup Lime Juice

1/4 tsp Salt

1/4 tsp Ground Pepper

DIRECTIONS

Sauce your 'meat' of choice using the SAUTÉ MODE and LESS setting of the Instant Pot.

Add the Garlic Powder, Onion Powder, Chili Powder, & Cumin and stir frequently until lightly browned

Use a little veggie broth to keep it from sticking

Remove from pot and set aside

Sauté onion, carrots, and celery on SAUTÉ MODE and LESS setting until soft and translucent

Use Veg Broth as needed to keep from sticking

Be sure and scrape up any browned bits on bottom of pot as these add to the flavor

Add minced garlic and stir for 1 minute

Turn off the Instant Pot

Add Veggie Broth, Water, Oregano, and dried Beans

Attach lid, set to SEALING, and select MANUAL mode for 30 minutes

After time is up, allow to vent naturally for 10 minutes and then use quick release

Stir broth and add potatoes, chilis, tomatoes, and the "meat" you set aside

Attach lid, set to SEALING, select MANUAL mode and 8 minutes

After time is up, allow to vent naturally for 5 minutes then quick release

Stir in Lime Juice

Stir in Masa Flour - 1 Tbs at a time, until desired thickness - up to 3 Tbs

Apple Spice Beef Stew

Total Time: 45 mins

Servings: 5-6

INGREDIENTS

2.2 Lbs. grass fed beef - cut into bite size chunks

2 apples - any variety - rough chop

1 large white onion - rough chop

3 or 4 large carrots - bite size chunks

2 T garlic flakes - or - 1 1/2 T powder

1 t cinnamon powder

1/4 t cloves powder

1 T dried Oregano

1 t sea salt

1 1/2 cup homemade broth

DIRECTIONS

Brown onion and meat in the instant pot with about 1T olive oil until meat is no longer pink (sauté setting) - about 5-6 minutes

Add spices and continue cooking on sauté for 2-3 minutes

Add remaining ingredients, seal the pot, set to high pressure and cook for 22 minutes

Quick release and serve

Serve as is, or alongside a baked sweet potato or on top of some cassava mash.

Beef Luau Stew

Total Time: 25 mins

Servings: 1-2

INGREDIENTS

Luau leaves (taro leaves) stems & fibrous veins removed

8 cups water

Hawaiian salt

3 lb chuck roast

1/2 onion

2 tbsp minced garlic

4 cups chicken broth

2 cans coconut milk

Salt & pepper to taste

DIRECTIONS

Cleaned and cut off stems of luau leaves. Chop leaves and add to pot with 8 cups water. Sprinkle some Hawaiian salt and push leaves into water.

Cook on manual for 15 min. Let Natural Pressure Release for 10, then quick release. Drain leaves.

Cut chuck roast into big chunks. Sauté meat with coconut oil. Add sliced onions, garlic, 4 cups chicken broth, and cooked luau leaves. Stir to incorporate. Cancel sauté and cook on Meat/Stew for 25 min. Let Natural Pressure Release for 10 min, then quick release.

Cancel keep warm and hit sauté. Add two cans of coconut milk and stir. Season to taste.

Italian Sausage Stew

Total Time: 10 mins

Servings: 1-2

INGREDIENTS

2 TB butter to cook in

½ lb pastured ground pork

½ tsp onion powder

½ tsp garlic powder

1½ tsp basil

½ tsp thyme

¼ tsp cumin

½ tsp marjoram

¼ tsp cayenne

1 tsp sea salt

¼ tsp black pepper

1 medium onion, diced

2 carrots, diced

2 stalks of celery, diced

4 cloves of garlic, minced

½ cup white wine

1 - 15oz can organic diced tomatoes

2 quarts bone broth

2-3 large handfuls kale, chopped

8oz gluten free noodles

Sea salt/pepper to taste

Freshly grated parm or other raw cheese to garnish

DIRECTIONS

Set the Instant Pot to "sauté". Once the bottom is warm put butter in to melt and then add the pork and all of the seasonings. Stir to combine and brown the meat.

Add the onion, carrot, celery, and garlic, combine and cook for 5-7 minutes until the veggies are soft and sweet.

Add the white wine to deglaze the pan scraping up any bits at the bottom.

Add the diced tomatoes, broth, kale and noodles and stir to combine. Put the Instant Pot lid on, make sure the valve is sealed and pressure cook for 3 minutes. Release the valve, season with salt and pepper to taste and serve with freshly grated parmesan.

Beef and Garlic Stew

Total Time: 1 hr 10 mins

Servings: 1-2

INGREDIENTS

3 lbs stew beef (or chuck roast or short ribs, see note below), cut into chunks

1/2 tsp salt

1/2 tsp black pepper

2 tbsp white rice flour (optional)

2 tbsp ghee

1/2 onion, diced

2 cloves garlic, minced

2 tbsp tomato paste

3/4 cup red wine (Zinfandel, Merlot, Cabernet Sauvignon)

3 cups beef broth

3 carrots, peeled and cut into chunks

3 parsnips, peeled and cut into chunks

3 celery stalks, cut into chunks

1.5 lbs waxy potatoes (red, golden, etc), cut into chunks

3 sprigs fresh thyme (1/2 tsp dried okay)

salt and pepper to taste

1 small handful parsley, chopped

Directions

Combine the beef, salt, pepper, and rice flour; toss to dust the beef evenly.

Plug in your Instant Pot and press the "Sauté" button. Add the ghee and warm until melted and shimmering, about 3 minutes. Add 1/3 of the beef and sauté until browned, about 6 minutes, then remove the beef and add another 1/3 of the beef. Continue until the rest of the beef has cooked, about 20 minutes total; set the beef aside.

Add the onion and sauté until softened, about 4 minutes, and then add the garlic and tomato paste. Sauté until aromatic, about 30 seconds, then add the wine and broth. Bring to a simmer, scraping up any browned bits from the bottom of the pot. Add the beef (and any accumulated juices), carrots, parsnips, celery, potatoes, and thyme.

Cover and set the Instant Pot to "Meat/Stew" (high pressure) for 20 minutes. Once the Instant Pot finishes, wait until it depressurizes, about 15 minutes. You'll know it's ready when you can remove the lid easily.

Gently remove the solid ingredients from the pot (the carrots and parsnips will be very tender) and set aside. Set the Instant Pot to "Sauté" again and simmer the sauce until reduced by half, about 10 minutes. Taste and add salt or pepper if needed. Return the solid ingredients to the pot, stir in the chopped parsley, and then serve.

Korean Chicken Stew

Total Time: 1 hr

Servings: 4

INGREDIENTS

3 lbs of bone-in skinless chicken thighs (about 8-10 thighs)

2 medium carrots cut into large chunks

2 white potatoes cut into large chunks

4 shiitake mushrooms sliced

4 minced garlic cloves

1 yellow onion sliced

2 green onions, sliced thinly (for garnish)

1 cup of sweet potato noodles, soaked in warm water for 30 minutes (optional)

sprinkle of sesame seeds for garnish

1 red hot pepper sliced (optional, if you want some spice)

salt and pepper

small amount of cooking oil

For the sauce

1/2 cup of soy sauce

2 tablespoons of brown sugar

2 tablespoons of oyster sauce

2 tablespoons of rice wine (mirin)

1 tablespoon of sesame oil

1/2 inch of grated ginger

DIRECTIONS

Prepare your vegetables

Slice your onions, and cut your carrots/potatoes into large pieces as shown. Slice your shiitake mushrooms, and optional red chili if you choose. Slice your green onions as shown for garnish. Set aside.

Slice onions

Cut carrots into chunks

Cut potatoes into large chunks

Slice shitake mushrooms

(optional) Sliced red hot pepper

Slice green onions lengthwise

Prepare your sauce

Combine your ingredients for the sauce, and mix well.

Mix your sauce

Your prepped ingredients

Press the SAUTÉ button on your Instant Pot. When the display reads HOT, add about a tablespoon of cooking oil. Brown each side of the chicken, about 1 minute both sides. While doing this, salt and pepper both sides. Do this in batches so you don't overcrowd the pot. Remove the chicken. Add the garlic and onions (and optional chili if you want extra spice) and cook until translucent, about 2 minutes. Put the chicken back in the pot. Add the vegetables on top of the chicken, then pour the sauce over everything. Close the pot lid. Press CANCEL to stop the sauté process.

Brown your chicken on SAUTÉ mode

Don't forget the salt and pepper

remove chicken then add

Add chicken and vegetables

Pour sauce on top

close the lid

Press POULTRY, then press the - (minus) button until the display reads 12. Make sure the pressure valve is in the SEALING position. The timer will start to count down once the float valve pops up. NOTE: if you are using skinless BONELESS chicken thighs, reduce your time to 10 minutes.

Once the timer is done, open your pressure valve to VENTING to release the pressure. Once the float valve drops, open the lid and take out the chicken and vegetables from the pot into a serving dish. Add your sweet potato noodles to the leftover liquid in the pot. Press CANCEL, to stop the keep warm function.

Press SAUTÉ to heat the sauce up to a boil. The noodles will finish cooking in about 2 minutes. Press CANCEL once you're done to turn your Instant Pot off. Spoon the noodles over the vegetables and chicken. Pour any leftover sauce on top of the dish. Add your green onions and sesame seeds on top for garnish. Enjoy this dish with rice!

Goat Stew

Total Time: 1 hr 10 mins

Servings: 2-4

INGREDIENTS

1 lb frozen bone-in goat meat (cubed)

1 rib celery, chopped

1 carrot, chopped

3 cloves garlic, minced

1 small onion, roughly chopped

4 oz. tomato paste

A dash of sherry wine or balsamic vinegar

1 cup chicken stock

½ cup water

2 tablespoons olive oil, divided

1 tablespoon cumin seeds, grounded

A few pinches of dried rosemary

Kosher salt

Pepper

Optional: roasted tomatoes

DIRECTIONS

Heat Instant Pot on Sauté Function, wait until it says Hot on the screen

Add 1 tablespoon of olive oil to the pot, add the frozen goat meat, add pinch of kosher salt and pepper

Cook and sear all sides of the goat meat, add grounded cumin seed and few pinches of dried rosemary spice

Stir occasionally for 2 minutes, remove the goat meat from the pot, set aside

Add 1 tablespoon of olive oil to the pot, add onion, add a pinch of kosher salt and pepper

Cook until onions are a bit soften and browned, add minced garlic, stir for 30 seconds

Add celery and carrot, add a pinch of kosher salt and pepper, stir and cook for 2 minutes

Add a dash of sherry wine and deglaze the pot, allow the wine to reduce

Add 1 cup of chicken stock and ½ cup of water, make sure the pot has been deglazed completely

Stir in the tomato paste, mix well, add the goat meat back to the pot, make sure the meat is spread out soaked in the sauce

Close the lid and set to Manual for 40 minutes cook time, natural release

(Optional) Add roasted tomatoes to the final dish - please taste and add more kosher salt. Serve.

Chicken Pot Pie Stew

Total Time: 50 mins

Servings: 6-8

INGREDIENTS

4 large frozen chicken breasts

1 large onion, chopped

1 bag of frozen mixed vegetables

salt and pepper

4 cups of chicken broth

1 cup heavy cream (or milk)

2 Tbsp. flour

DIRECTIONS

Put your frozen chicken breasts, chopped onion, salt and pepper and 4 cups of the chicken broth in to the Instant Pot.

Lock the lid and set your Instant Pot to the "Soup/Stew" setting and the timer for 30 minutes.

After 30 minutes, use the quick release to vent out the steam and open the pot, being careful to open the lid away from you since there is still steam inside and you don't want it rushing towards your face.

Remove the chicken breasts to a plate and allow cooling for a few minutes. Cut the chicken breasts into bite sized pieces and return to the pot.

Turn the Instant Pot to the "Sauté" setting so the broth will start boiling. Add your bag of frozen veggies and more broth if you need to (depend on how much of the veggies you add) and allow the mixture to come back up to a boil.

In a small bowl, mix the 1 cup of heavy cream with the flour and pour this in to the mix to help thicken the soup.

Taste and add more seasonings if you wish and then serve.

Beef and Butternut Squash Stew

Total Time: 45 mins

Servings: 10

INGREDIENTS

1 large onion chopped

2 cloves garlic minced

2 celery stalks chopped

2 carrots chopped

2 Tbsp tomato paste

1 tomato peeled and chopped

2 lbs beef stew cut in 1" pieces

4 Tbsp arrowroot starch

6 cups peeled and chopped butternut squash cut in 1" cubes

1/2 cup Marsala wine

2 1/2 cup beef broth

3 Tbsp olive oil

2 bay leaves

1 tsp sweet Hungarian paprika

1 tsp thyme

1 tsp rosemary

DIRECTIONS

Add 1 Tbsp olive oil to the instant pot. Add onions, garlic, celery, carrots, tomato and tomato paste to the pot. Season well with salt and freshly ground black pepper. Stir.

Season beef stew with salt, black pepper and 4 Tbsp of arrowroot starch (or cornstarch). Add beef and butternut squash to the pot. Season butternut squash with salt and freshly ground black pepper.

Season everything with sweet Hungarian paprika, thyme, rosemary and add 2 bay leaves. Stir everything. Pour wine and beef broth, and the remaining 2 Tbsp of the olive oil.

Plug the instant pot. Close the lid, and turn the valve to sealing. Press Meat/Stew button and cook on Normal/High Pressure for 30 minutes.

When it's ready, press Keep Warm/Cancel button and turn the steam release to venting (aka venting).

Japanese Pork Tender Rib Stew

Total Time: 60 mins

Servings: 2-3

INGREDIENTS

28 Oz. soft pork ribs

4 slices ginger

1 clove garlic, minced

3 Tbsp Japanese salt-reduced light soy sauce

2 Tbsp. mirin

1 Tbsp cooking rice wine

3 tsp white vinegar

½ Tbsp rock sugar, roughly pounded

1 cup water

14 oz. radish, peeled and roughly chopped

salt, to taste

spring onion, for garnish

2 tsp corn flour / corn starch

1 Tbsp water

DIRECTIONS

Blanch the pork ribs. Drain well. Set aside.

Use an Instant Pot (See instructions below for stovetop pot), press "Sauté" (medium) to heat oil. Brown the pork ribs on both sides in two batches. Return all the pork ribs into the pot.

Add in ginger, garlic, soy sauce, mirin, wine, vinegar, rock sugar and water. Cover and turn the steam release handle to the "sealing" position. Set "Meat/Stew", high pressure, for 35 minutes. When the program finishes, wait 5 minutes, then run quick pressure release carefully. After the float valve drops to the down position, you'll find the lid can be removed easily.

Add in the radish. Cover the lid with "sealing" position again. Press "Meat/Stew" and cook for another 10 minutes. Quickly release the pressure. When the valve drops, remove the lid and press "Sauté" button to reduce the sauce by 1/3. Season with salt.

Stir in the thickening and cook to your preferred consistency. Garnish with spring onion. Serve hot. Enjoy!

Kimchi Stew

Total Time: 60 mins

Servings: 4-6

INGREDIENTS

3 cups chopped sour kimchi - you can use more if you wish!

1/2 lb to 1 lb of pork belly cut into 1.5-inch sized pieces

1 medium onion - sliced

Small amount of cooking oil

1/4 cup of kimchi juice

2 tablespoons of red pepper paste

1 tablespoon of red pepper flakes (optional if you prefer your stew spicier)

1 tablespoon of sugar

4 cups of water

1 package of firm tofu

3 green onions chopped (for garnish)

1 teaspoon of sesame oil

Broth packet:

6 whole garlic cloves

4 small square (about 2 inches in length) sheets of dried kelp

6-8 dried anchovies

DIRECTIONS

Slice your onions, green onions, and your pork belly (or pork shoulder). Slice the tofu. Prepare the broth packet by using either a disposable tea packet (as shown below), or a tea seeper. Place the garlic, dried kelp, and dried anchovies in the packet and set aside.

Slice onions

Chop green onions

Slice tofu

Broth packet or tea sipper

Dried kelp, dried anchovies

Broth packet

Press the sauté button on the instant pot. When the display reads hot, add your cooking oil.

Brown the pork for 2-3 minutes. Add your kimchi and onions. Continue to heat everything up for several minutes.

Add 4 cups of water and 1/4 cup kimchi juice (optional, add it if you have enough). Use hot water, this will make the instant pot come to pressure faster. Add the sugar, red pepper flakes, and red pepper paste. Close the instant pot. Press cancel, then meat/stew, set the timer for 20 minutes. Switch the valve to sealing.

Brown the pork on sauté mode

Add kimchi and onions

Add 4 cups water

Add kimchi juice

Add the ingredients

Close lid

When the timer has finished, switch the pressure valve to venting. After the float valve drops, open the Instant Pot.

Add the Broth packet, and the tofu. Use a spoon to press everything down into the broth. Close the Instant Pot. Press MEAT/STEW and set the timer for 3 minutes.

Set the pressure valve to SEALING. Once the timer finishes, switch the pressure valve to VENTING. After the float valve drops, open the Instant Pot. Remove the broth packet and discard. Add sesame oil. When you are ready to serve, add the green onions on top. Serve with rice.

Spicy Beef Stew

Total Time: 45 mins

Servings: 4

INGREDIENTS

2 tbsp ghee or avocado oil

1 lb beef stew meat, cut into cubes

1 onion, diced

3 medium potatoes, chopped

4 carrots, chopped

2 celery stalks, chopped

2 cups kale leaves, stems removed

1 tsp garlic powder

½ tsp black pepper

2 cups bone broth

2 tbsp your favorite hot sauce

Sea salt, to taste

DIRECTIONS

Set your Instant Pot to Sauté setting and add avocado oil.

Add the meat and stir until the meat is browned.

Add and stir in the rest of the ingredient, except salt.

Close the lid, and make sure the pressure valve is set to "sealing."

Set the Instant Pot to Meat/Stew.

Once finished, about 40 minutes, the Instant Pot will beep. If you are eating right away, hit "Cancel" then release the pressure valve, making sure your hand is away from the opening where the steam escapes. If not, the Instant Pot will automatically switch to the "Warm" setting for the next 10 hours and the pressure will slowly lower on its own.

Taste and salt, if necessary.

Chicken and Sweet Potato Stew

Total Time: 15 mins

Servings: 1-2

INGREDIENTS

2 Cloves grated garlic

1 Tbsp grape seed oil (or any cooking oil)

1 Star anise

3 Cloves

2 Bay leaves

1 Stick of cinnamon

2 Green chilies - slit

1 Tsp of whole peppercorns

3 Cardamom pods

2 Lb Chicken (on the bone gives more flavor but boneless is fine)

1 Large sweet potato - cubed

1 Medium red onion - finely sliced

1 Tomato - finely chopped

2 Cups water

Salt to taste

A pinch of sugar (optional)

1 Tsp of butter or ghee

DIRECTIONS

Put oil in an Instant Pot, add the garlic, then all the whole spices and sauté.

Add the onions and tomatoes and green chilies and sauté till the onions lose their color.

Add all the chicken pieces and cook till they lose the raw look.

Add the water, cover and let simmer till chicken and potatoes are cooked. If using the IP then cook in 'poultry' mode.

Once ready, add salt and pinch of sugar.

Mung Bean Stew

Total Time: 30 mins

Servings: 1-2

INGREDIENTS

3/4 cup mung beans

½ brown basmati rice

½ tsp coconut oil

½ tsp cumin seeds

½ red onion, chopped

1 can (28 oz of crushed tomatoes)

5 cloves of garlic

1 inch ginger, peeled

1 tsp turmeric

1 tsp ground coriander

½ tsp garam masala

½ tsp cayenne

¼ tsp black pepper

4 cups water

1 tsp lemon juice

¾ to 1¼ tsp salt

DIRECTIONS

Soke the Mung Beans overnight in a bowl of water. Soak the brown rice for 15 minutes.

Into a blender or Vitamix, blend onions, tomatoes, garlic, ginger, spices and 2 tbl of water and blend on setting 5 with a few pulses.

Start the Instant Pot on the Sauté setting. Once hot, add some oil and toast up the cumin seeds for about 1 minute. Then proceed to add the puree from the blender and cook for 15 minutes until it thickens up. Then turn the Instant Pot off.

Drain the beans and rice and add to the Instant Pot. Add your water, salt and juice. Stir well and add the lid. Close the vent. Using the manual button, add 15 minutes to the timer and let the machine go. Let the Instant Pot release naturally in approximately 10 minutes. Serve with your favorite bread, Naan or crackers.

Italian Chickpea Stew

Total Time: 40 mins

Servings: 4

INGREDIENTS

For the pesto

1 1/2 packed cups fresh basil leaves (about 3/4 ounce)

1/4 cup extra-virgin olive oil, plus additional if needed

1/4 cup grated Parmesan cheese (about 1 ounce)

1 garlic clove, minced

1 tablespoon toasted pine nuts

For the chickpeas

1 tablespoon plus 1/2 teaspoon kosher salt, divided

4 cups of water

12 ounces dried chickpeas

2 tablespoons extra-virgin olive oil

1 small onion, chopped (about 3/4 cup)

2 medium carrots, peeled and chopped (about 3/4 cup)

1 (14-ounce) can diced tomatoes, undrained

4 cups chicken stock

1/4 cup grated Parmesan or similar cheese

DIRECTIONS

Make the pesto: Combine the basil, oil, cheese, garlic, and pine nuts in a small food processor or blender. Pulse until a coarse paste forms, adding a tablespoon or two of water or more olive oil, if necessary to get a loose-enough consistency. Set aside 1/3 cup of pesto for this recipe; the remainder can be refrigerated in an airtight container for a week or so, or frozen for several months.

Soak the chickpeas: In a large bowl, dissolve 1 tablespoon of kosher salt in the water. Add the chickpeas and soak at room temperature for 8 to 24 hours. Drain and rinse.

Sauté the onions: Preheat the Instant Pot by selecting Sauté and adjust to More for high heat. Add the olive oil and heat until it shimmers. Add the onion and sprinkle with 1/4 teaspoon of salt. Cook, stirring frequently, until the onion pieces separate and soften, 2 to 3 minutes.

Pressure cook: Add the drained chickpeas, carrots, tomatoes with their juice, stock, and remaining 1/4 teaspoon of salt. Lock the lid into place. Select Manual; adjust the pressure to High and the time to 10 minutes. After cooking, naturally release the pressure for 10 minutes, then quick release any remaining pressure. Unlock and remove the lid.

Serve the chickpeas: Ladle the chickpeas into bowls and top each with a spoonful of pesto. Sprinkle with the cheese and serve.

Veggie Stew

Total Time: 45 mins

Servings: 8

INGREDIENTS

1/2 med Onion (minced)

1 stalk Celery (minced)

1 med Carrot (minced)

2 cloves Garlic (minced)

1/4 cup Vegetable Broth (low sodium)

8 oz White Button Mushrooms

8 oz Portobello Mushrooms (chopped)

1 tsp Italian Seasoning

1 tsp Rosemary

1/2 tsp Rubbed Sage

1/2 cup Red Wine

1 can Diced Tomatoes (15oz)

1 can Tomato Sauce (8oz)

3 cups Vegetable Broth (Low Sodium)

2 med Carrots (diced)

1 stalk Celery (diced)

1 cup Green Beans (frozen or fresh) (diced)

2 med Yukon Gold Potatoes (diced)

1 Tbs Balsamic Vinegar

1/2 tsp Salt

1/2 tsp Kitchen Bouquet

1/4 tsp Ground Pepper

3/4 cup Pearl Onions

4 oz Frozen Peas

2 Tbs Corn Starch

DIRECTIONS

Set the Instant Pot to SAUTÉ mode and select LESS.

Sauté first 4 ingredients (onion, celery, carrot, and garlic) until soft and translucent

Add Italian Seasoning, Rosemary, and Sage

Add mushrooms and sauté until all liquid has evaporated

(It's ok if veggies slightly brown and stick a little)

Deglaze pan with Red Wine, scraping up any bits on the bottom.

Add Tomatoes, Tomato Sauce, and Vegetable Broth

Add all remaining veggies except Pearl Onions and Peas

Add seasonings

Attach lid to Instant Pot,

Ensure Release Valve is set to SEALING,

Press MANUAL MODE and set timer to 15 minutes

Once finished, cover steam release with towel and CAREFULLY release all pressure

Remove lid and stir in pearl onions, peas, and corn starch slurry

Stir and serve.

Chicken Stew

Total Time: 30 mins

Servings: 6

INGREDIENTS

1 tbs olive oil

1 onion chopped

1/2 red pepper chopped

1/2 yellow pepper chopped

1 1/2 lb potatoes peeled and chopped

1/2 lb green beans chopped

1/2 cup kalamata olives cut in half

2 cups chicken broth

1 lb chicken breast

1/2 tsp oregano

1/2 tsp cumin

1/8 tsp cinnamon

1/2 tsp salt

1/2 tsp pepper

Fresh basil for garnish optional

DIRECTIONS

Set the Instant Pot to Sauté, and once it's hot, add the olive oil and onion. Cook for a minute, and then add the red and yellow peppers. Cook for a couple more minutes, stirring occasionally, until crisp tender.

Add the potatoes, green beans, olives, and broth to the pot. Place the chicken on top, and sprinkle it with the seasonings.

Cook the stew on manual high pressure for 8 to 10 minutes (8 minutes for thin chicken breast, 10 minutes for thick chicken breast). Use a quick release to open the pot, and use a meat thermometer to check the temperature of the thickest part of the chicken. If it hasn't yet reached 165 degrees, set the pot to Sauté and cook for another minute or two as needed.

Once the chicken is fully cooked, remove it from the pot and chop it into bite-sized pieces. Return the chicken to the pot and stir. Garnish with fresh basil if desired, and serve warm.

Quinoa

Total Time: 5 mins

Servings: 1-2

INGREDIENTS

1 cup dry quinoa

1 cup water

DIRECTIONS

Measure out desired amount of quinoa. I have made anywhere from 1 to 3 cups (dry measurement).

Rinse the quinoa, using a fine mesh strainer

This Instant Pot quinoa is my go-to method for cooking quinoa, and it is super simple and quick.

Add rinsed and drained quinoa to the inner stainless-steel pot. Add an equal amount of water for a 1:1 ratio

Place the lid on, lock it, and place the lever on "cooking," and cook on manual high pressure for 1 minute.

Allow the pressure to release naturally (NPR).

After the pressure indicator pin drops, your quinoa is ready. Fluff with a fork, and it is ready to be eaten.

Black Beans

Total Time: 50 mins

Servings: 12

INGREDIENTS

2 1/2 Tablespoons Better than Bullion Vegetable Base

1 pound dry black beans

5 1/2 cups water

1/2 teaspoon garlic powder

1/2 teaspoon coriander

1/2 teaspoon cumin

1/2 teaspoon paprika

Get Ingredients Powered by Chicory

DIRECTIONS

Rinse the dry beans off, and drain off the excess liquid.

Add the beans to the pot, plus the 5 1/2 cups water, vegetable base and all spices.

Cook on manual high pressure for 50 minutes, and let the pressure naturally (NPR). In other words, wait for the pin to drop without using the quick release lever. Mine took about 25 minutes, FYI.

Taste to see if you want to add any more salt or pepper. The BTB vegetable base is plenty salty enough for us, but feels free to add more to taste.

Serve in burritos, tacos, over rice or as a side item.

Jasmine Rice

Total Time: 20 mins

Servings: 4-6

INGREDIENTS

2 cups uncooked jasmine rice (water to rice ration is 1:1)

2 cups water

DIRECTIONS

Using a fine mesh strainer, rinse the rice well and drain.

Add the rinsed rice to the pot, along with an equal amount of water.

Cook on high manual pressure for 10 minutes.

Allow the pot to release naturally.

Fluff with a fork and serve immediately.

Potato Salad

Total Time: 20 mins

Servings: 6-8

INGREDIENTS

1 cup water

2 pounds red potatoes, diced

3 eggs

1/2 cup mayonnaise (I recommend Trader Joe's, Duke's or Hellmann's)

1/4 cup sweet pickle relish

1/4 cup Dijon or spicy brown mustard (I am using Trader Joe's spicy brown)

1 Tablespoon honey

2 Tablespoons apple cider vinegar

1/4 teaspoon garlic powder

salt and pepper, to taste

Optional garnishes: chopped fresh parsley or diced green onions)

DIRECTIONS

Add one cup of water to the Instant Pot, and place a steamer basket on top.

Place the diced potatoes in the steamer basket, and arrange the eggs on top.

Place the lid on, and lock it, and cook for 5 minutes on manual high pressure.

While the potatoes and eggs are cooking, go ahead and whisk together the mayo, mustard, honey, sweet pickle relish, apple cider vinegar in a large mixing bowl (Note: we will be adding the potatoes and eggs later).

Add a pinch of salt and pepper to the dressing, whisk to combine and set aside.

Once the 5 minutes of manual high pressure are complete, allow the pot to naturally release for 5 additional minutes, and the quick release the remaining pressure after that.

Place the eggs in an ice water bath to cool them and stop the cooking.

Carefully add the hot potatoes to the larger mixing bowl on top of the dressing.

Add the garlic powder, plus about 1/2 teaspoon of salt and 1/4 teaspoon pepper on top of the potatoes.

After the eggs have cooled for about 3 to five minutes, peel them, dice them to desired size, and add them to the large mixing bowl, on top of the potatoes.

Stir everything to combine until everything is coated with the dressing.

Taste to check your salt and pepper preference; add more if desired.

Refrigerate to cool.

Wild Rice Pilaf

Total Time: 30 mins

Servings: 8

INGREDIENTS

1 2/3 Tablespoon oil

1 yellow onion, diced

2 cups sliced mushrooms of your choice

2 cloves garlic, finely minced

2 cups wild rice and brown rice medley, rinsed and drained

2.5 cups water

2 1/2 teaspoons Better Than Bullion Vegetable Base

1/4 cup chopped fresh parsley

salt and pepper to taste

DIRECTIONS

Preheat the Instant Pot on sauté setting (regular), and add oil to the pot.

After about a minute, add the onion and mushrooms, and cook for about 4 minutes, stirring frequently.

Add the garlic, and cook 30 seconds more.

Add the rice, and toast for 2 to 3 minutes, stirring constantly.

Turn off the heat, add the water and Better Than Bullion vegetable base, and scrape to remove any rice that stuck to the bottom or sides.

Place the lid on, lock it, and cook at high manual pressure for 20 minutes, and allow the pot to NPR.

Once the pressure has released, turn off the pot (so rice doesn't scorch), remove the lid, fluff with a fork, and taste to see if you need to add salt. This will largely depend on how salty your stock/ broth was.

Add (optional) chopped fresh parsley for garnish, and serve immediately.

Pinto Beans

Total Time: 45 mins

Servings: 8

INGREDIENTS

1 pound dry pinto beans

5 1/2 cups water

1 2/3 Tablespoon Better Than Bullion vegetable base

salt and pepper to taste

DIRECTIONS

Rinse off your pinto beans, and drain them using a wire mesh strainer.

Add them to the Instant Pot, along with the water and Better Than Bullion vegetable base.

Close and lock the lid, and cook on manual high pressure for 45 minutes.

Allow the pressure to naturally release.

Black Bean Soup

Total Time: 45 mins

Servings: 8

INGREDIENTS

1 medium onion, diced

1 red bell pepper, diced

1 green bell pepper, diced

1 can diced tomatoes, undrained (14.5 ounce)

3 stalks celery, diced

1 pound of dry black beans, rinsed

1 teaspoon salt

1/2 teaspoon black pepper (more or less, to taste)

1 teaspoon hot sauce

1 Tablespoon paprika

2 Tablespoons chili powder

2 Tablespoons cumin

2 bay leaves

6 cups vegetable stock or broth (omnivores may substitute chicken broth, if you wish)

DIRECTIONS

Add all ingredients (except toppings) to the Instant Pot, and place the lid on top, with the vent set to "sealing."

Cook the soup on manual high pressure for 40 minutes, and let the pressure naturally release. Plan on the whole cooking time being over an hour.

After the pot is depressurized, remove the lid, and carefully remove the bay leaves.

Serve with desired toppings: squeeze of lime, cilantro, diced avocado, green onions, tortilla chips, etc.

Black-Eyed Peas and Ham

Total Time: 30 mins

Servings: 10

INGREDIENTS

1 pound of dried black-eyed peas (rinsed, but not pre-soaked)

6.5 cups stock

5 ounces diced ham

DIRECTIONS

Add all ingredients to the Instant Pot, place the lid on and lock it.

Cook for 30 minutes at high manual pressure.

Allow the pot to release naturally.

Salt and pepper to taste.

Ham and Bean Soup

Total Time: 1 hr

Servings: 8

INGREDIENTS

1 20-ounce pack Hurst dry beans (15 beans soup mix) rinsed, discard the spice packet

1 onion diced

2 cloves garlic minced

2 leaves bay

1 Tablespoon fresh thyme

7.5 cups chicken stock

1 teaspoon hot sauce

1 lb diced ham can use leftover

salt and pepper to taste

DIRECTIONS

Place all ingredients (except salt and pepper) in the Instant Pot.

For the Instant Pot, cook on high manual pressure for 40 minutes with natural pressure release (do not use the quick release valve, but let the pressure indicator lower on its own).

Salt and pepper, to taste. I always taste the soup before I add salt and pepper. There is already a fair amount of salt in the ham and the broth, so sometimes I don't need it at all.

Beef Chili

Total Time: 1 hr.

Servings: 6

INGREDIENTS

1 pound of ground beef 85% lean

1 small to medium yellow onion diced

1 bell pepper diced, red or green

3 cloves medium fresh garlic finely minced

1 tablespoons chili powder

2/3 tablespoon cumin

1 teaspoons ground coriander

1/2 tablespoon real maple syrup

1/2 teaspoon salt

1/4 teaspoon black pepper

1 teaspoons hot sauce

1/3 cup red wine

2 cans kidney beans undrained, 14.5 ounces

1 can diced tomatoes undrained, 14.5 ounces

1 can can green chilis undrained, 4 ounces

1/4 cup organic ketchup

DIRECTIONS

Spray the Instant Pot with a little cooking spray, or drizzle with a little oil.

Set to sauté on regular (middle heat setting), and give it a minute to heat up.

Add beef, and brown for about 5 minutes, breaking it apart with a wooden spoon.

Add onions and peppers, garlic, spices, wine/broth, maple syrup, salt and pepper.

Cook for about 8 to 10 minutes.

Turn off the heat, and stir in the tomatoes, green chiles, beans, ketchup and hot sauce.

Add salt and pepper to taste.

Place the lid on, and lock it, with the vent set to "sealing."

Use the manual buttons to set it to 12 minutes.

Allow the pressure cooked to release naturally. Do not use the quick release lever, but let the pressure indicator sink on its own. Mine took about 23 minutes.

After pressure indicator has lowered, switch the lever to venting, and remove the lid.

Optional: If you wish to reduce the liquids, you can cook on sauté low for a few more minutes, until some of the liquids evaporate. Stir frequently, if you do this.

Chicken Noodle Soup

Total Time: 35 mins

Servings: 6

INGREDIENTS

1/2 tablespoon of olive or cooking spray

1/2 cup diced onion about half of a large onion

3 stalks of celery chopped

3 carrots chopped

2 cloves of fresh garlic minced

2 leaves bay

1/2 Tablespoon fresh parsley chopped

7 cups chicken stock homemade or store-bought

6 ounces uncooked egg noodle pasta

6 ounces of cooked shredded chicken

salt and pepper to taste

DIRECTIONS

Drizzle the oil into the inner stainless-steel pot, and preheat on the sauté setting to medium for about a minute.

Add the bay leaves, parsley, onion, celery and carrots and cook for about 3 to 5 minutes, until they start to get tender.

Add the garlic, and cook a minute more.

Turn off the heat, add the chicken stock, cooked shredded chicken and pasta.

Place the lid on top, lock it, and use the manual setting to set to 3 minutes high pressure.

Allow the pressure to naturally release for 8 minutes, then quick release it to release the rest of the pressure.

Cilantro Lime Rice

Total Time: 3 mins

Servings: 6

INGREDIENTS

1 cup brown basmati rice uncooked

2 cups water (adjust water ratio for other types of rice)

1/4 teaspoon salt (plus more to taste)

Juice of 1/2 lime

1.5 tablespoons butter

1/2 cup frozen corn kernels optional

1/4 cup cilantro chopped

DIRECTIONS

Prepare 1 cup (dry) any type of rice plus salt, using the proportions, times, water prescribed in the Instant Pot recipe book.

When rice is cooked, stir in the lime juice, butter and cilantro.

Serve immediately.

Delicious Chicken Noodle Soup

Total Time: 50 mins

Servings: 2-4

INGREDIENTS

1 tablespoon of olive oil

1 small onion, diced

3 cloves of garlic, minced

5 carrots, peeled and sliced into 1/2 inch pieces

2 celery sticks, sliced into 1/2 inch pieces

1 whole 5 pound chicken, giblets removed and discarded

2 tablespoon of soy sauce8 cups of water

Kosher salt and freshly ground pepper

4 ounces of extra wide egg noodles

1/4 cup of minced fresh flat leaf parsley

DIRECTIONS

Set Instant Pot to Sauté function.

Heat olive oil and onions until onions start to soften and become translucent, 2-3 minutes.

Add garlic, carrots and celery and sauté for another minute.

Add whole chicken to Instant Pot, followed by water, soy sauce, 2 teaspoons of salt and several turns of freshly ground pepper.

Turn off Sauté function, lock Instant Pot lid in place, make sure pressure valve is set to sealing and set Instant Pot to High Pressure for 20 minutes, via manual mode.

Instant Pot will take 15-20 minutes to come to pressure, and then will countdown from 20 minutes.

After 20 minutes at high pressure, Instant Pot will beep and switch to keep warm mode.

Turn pressure release valve to Quick Release pressure.

Carefully open Instant Pot, keeping lid angled away from you to avoid very hot steam.

Remove whole chicken and set aside to shred.

Turn Instant Pot back to Sauté function and let chicken broth come to a boil.

Stir in egg noodles and let cook for about 5 minutes.

While noodles are cooking, shred chicken into bite sized pieces discarding bones and skin.

Once noodles are cooked, stir in chicken meat and fresh parsley.

Adjust salt and pepper to taste.

Buffalo Chicken

Total Time: 50 mins

Servings: 1-2

INGREDIENTS

1 pound of organic pasture raised chicken breast

1 onion, diced

3 tablespoons dairy free butter, ghee, or vegan butter (divided)

3 tablespoons buffalo sauce

16 ounces sweet potatoes, diced

1/2 teaspoon (or more) onion powder

1/2 teaspoon (or more) garlic powder

Sea salt and pepper to taste

DIRECTIONS

Using the "Sauté" feature on your Instant Pot, cook the onion in 1 tablespoon of the cooking fat.

Once nicely browned, place your chicken, sweet potatoes, remaining butter or ghee, buffalo sauce, and spices into the pot.

Secure the lid and use the "Poultry" feature. If your breasts are extra big and juicy (no offense) you may need 18 minutes. If you are using frozen chicken, you will need to cook for 30 minutes so you can select the "Manual" setting, using high pressure for 30 minutes.

Make sure the steam vent is closed and allow cooking for allotted time.

Once complete, quick release the steam vent and then remove the lid and serve.

If you'd like to thicken the sauce, you can make a slurry with 1-2 tablespoons of arrowroot or cassava flour and then reintroduce to the hot Instant Pot and stir.

Lentil Tortilla Soup

Total Time: 50 mins

Servings: 6

INGREDIENTS

1 cup diced onion

1 tsp avocado oil or olive oil

1 bell pepper, diced

1 jalapeno pepper, diced

2.5 cups vegetable broth

1 can (14-15 oz) tomato sauce or crushed tomatoes, extra to taste

1/2 cup salsa verde

1 tbsp tomato paste

1 (15 oz) can black beans, drained + rinsed

1 (15 oz) can pinto beans, drained + rinsed

1 cup corn (fresh, canned, or frozen)

3/4 cup dried red lentils

1/2 tsp chili powder

1/2 tsp garlic powder

1/2 tsp cumin

1/4 tsp cayenne pepper

1/4-1/2 cup heavy cream (optional)

Salt and pepper to taste

Crushed tortilla chips

Shredded cheddar cheese

Sliced or diced jalapenos

Chopped red onion

Fresh Pico de Gallo

Sliced avocado

Fresh cilantro

Sour cream or Greek Yogurt

DIRECTIONS

Chop your veggies and measure out the ingredients.

Next add everything but the heavy cream your toppings.

Allow natural pressure release.

Stir in the cream, add all your favorite toppings, and enjoy!

Squash Beef Stew

Total Time: 36 mins

Servings: 6

INGREDIENTS

4 tablespoons flour, divided

1 ½ teaspoons kosher salt and freshly ground black pepper

1 ½ teaspoon garlic salt

1 ½ teaspoons freshly ground black pepper

2 pounds beef chuck cut into cubes

3 tablespoons vegetable oil, divided

4 cloves garlic, pressed or minced

1 large onion, chopped, about 2 cups

3 ribs celery, chopped, about 1 cup

1 cup red wine

2 cups beef broth

1 tablespoon beef base

2 cups chopped carrots

1 pound of cremini or brown mushrooms, quartered

12 ounces butternut squash, cubed

2 cups quartered new red potatoes

2 bay leaves

6 thyme stems

DIRECTIONS

Place 2 tablespoons flour, kosher salt, garlic salt and freshly ground black pepper in a gallon freezer bag and toss to mix.

Add the beef chuck cubes to the freezer bag and toss the cubes in the flour mixture to coat.

Press sauté and heat 1 tablespoon of the oil. Add half of the floured beef cubes to the oil and brown the beef on all sides.

Transfer the beef to a bowl. Add another tablespoon of oil to the pot and brown the rest of the meat on all sides.

Add the garlic to the beef and cook for 30 seconds to 1 minute or until garlic becomes fragrant. Add this beef to the bowl.

Add the remaining tablespoon of oil to the pot and cook the onion and celery for 4-5 minutes or until softened, then add to the bowl with the beef.

Add the wine to the Instant Pot and bring to a boil, scraping the bits from the bottom of the cooker. Add the beef broth and the beef base to the Instant Pot and mix with the remaining 2 tablespoons of flour.

Add the butternut squash, carrots, red potatoes and mushrooms to the pot with the bay leaves and thyme. Seal the Instant Pot and set to the Stew setting and cook for 30 minutes.

Natural release, remove the bay leaves and serve.

Greek Pork Pitas

Total Time: 50 mins

Servings: 6-8

INGREDIENTS

Greek Pork:

3 pounds pork shoulder, fat trimmed

1 onion, chopped

3 cloves garlic, minced

1 tablespoon oregano

1 teaspoon salt

1 teaspoon onion powder

1 teaspoon black pepper

For the Pitas:

Pitas

Tzatziki

Toppings such as lettuce, tomatoes, red onion, feta, lemon, etc.

DIRECTIONS

Place all ingredients for the pork in an Instant Pot on the meat/stew setting (about 45 minutes).

Shred the meat and stir to mix in juices.

Cauliflower Soup

Total Time: 30 mins

Servings: 4

INGREDIENTS

For the salad:

1 tablespoon coconut oil

1 white onion

3 cloves garlic

1 extra-large or 2 medium sized fennel bulbs, stalks and fronds removed

1 pound of cauliflower florets

1 cup coconut milk

3 cups broth (bone broth or vegetable broth)

2 teaspoons salt

Optional: Truffle oil, for serving

Optional: Black pepper for serving

DIRECTIONS

Slice the onions, mince the garlic, and chop the fennel. If your cauliflower is not already chopped into florets, do that now. In the bottom of your instant pot, heat up the coconut oil. Sauté the onions until translucent. Add the garlic, fennel, and cauliflower. Sauté for 5-10 minutes, until the edges of the vegetables begin to turn golden.

Pour the broth and coconut milk into the pot. Add salt. Cook on the soup setting for at least 5 minutes.

Once the instant pot is done cooking, release the pressure and remove the lid. Use a standing blender or an immersion blender to puree the soup to a smooth, creamy consistency.

Scoop into serving bowls and drizzle with truffle oil. Top with freshly cracked pepper, and garnish with a left-over fennel frond. Serve hot.

Beef Drip Sandwiches

Total Time: 1 hr 15 mins

Servings: 8

INGREDIENTS

2 lb lean beef eye round roast

1 onion, chopped

1 cup beef broth

8 oz pepperoncini with juice, jarred

1/2 tsp salt

3 tbsp Italian seasoning

8 reduced calorie hamburger rolls

1 green pepper, sliced

1 red pepper, sliced

1 cup part skim shredded mozzarella cheese

DIRECTIONS

Add the beef, onion, pepperoncini's, beef broth, salt, and Italian seasoning the Instant Pot.

Cover and cook on high for 1 hour. Carefully vent the Instant Pot and shred the beef using two forks.

Lightly toast each roll in the broiler. Top with beef, thinly sliced peppers, and two tablespoons of cheese.

Return to broiler and cook for about one minute until cheese melts.

Chicken and Smoked Sausage Stew

Total Time: 30 mins

Servings: 6

INGREDIENTS

1 pound of boneless, skinless chicken thighs

1 pound of Andouille pork sausage

1 tablespoon coconut oil

6 cups chopped tomatoes

1 medium white onion

2 stalks celery

3 bell peppers

2 large carrots

2 cups bone broth or water

1/4 cup parsley

6 cloves garlic

1 teaspoon salt

1 teaspoon thyme

1/2 teaspoon smoked paprika

1/2 teaspoon crushed red chili flakes

1/4 teaspoon black pepper

1/4 teaspoon cayenne

1 bay leaf

Optional: hot sauce to taste

DIRECTIONS

Heat the coconut oil in the bottom of the Instant Pot (on the Sauté setting). Add the chicken and sausage to the pan and cook through. While the meat cooks, slice the onion. Dice the bell peppers, and chop the carrots and celery. Remove the meat from the pot, and set aside for later use.

Sauté the vegetables in the bottom of the Instant Pot, stirring occasionally. Mince the garlic, and add it to the pan. Add the broth and chopped tomatoes. Bring the mixture to a simmer (the sauté function will do this automatically)

Once the chicken and sausage are cool enough to handle, slice them into bite-sized pieces. Return them to the pot, along with the spices. Mince the parsley now, and add that as well. Give the stew one stir and then lock the lid on. Turn the Instant Pot to the soup setting and cook for 5-10 minutes.

Serve warm with hot sauce to taste. Note: This recipe can be done in a regular soup pot, just increase the final cooking time in step 3 to 20 to 30 minute, until the vegetables are tender and the flavors have simmered together.

Beef Chili

Total Time: 35 mins

Servings: 1-2

INGREDIENTS

1 lb grass-fed organic beef

1 green bell pepper, seeded and diced

1 large onion, diced

4 large carrots, chopped small

26 oz finely chopped tomatoes

½ teaspoon ground black pepper

1 teaspoon sea salt

1 teaspoon onion powder

1 tablespoon chopped fresh parsley

1 tablespoon Worcestershire sauce

4 teaspoons chili powder

1 teaspoon paprika

1 teaspoon garlic powder

Pinch of cumin

Dairy-free sour cream

Diced onions

Sliced jalapenos

DIRECTIONS

Press the "Sauté" button on the Instant Pot, and add the ground beef to the pot and cook until brown.

Add the remaining ingredients, mix well, then cover and lock the lid.

Press the "Keep Warm/Cancel" button on the Instant Pot, then press the "Meat/Stew" button to begin the pressure cooking.

It will automatically be set for 35 minutes. Make sure the steam valve is closed.

Once the chili is done, the Instant Pot will automatically switch to the "Keep Warm" mode.

Allow the pressure to release naturally or use the quick release.

Onion Soup

Total Time: 25 mins

Servings: 1-2

INGREDIENTS

2 tbsp / 30 ml avocado oil, coconut oil or good quality lard

8 cups / 960 g yellow onions

1 tbsp / 15 ml balsamic vinegar

6 cups / 1.4 L pork stock

1 tsp / 5 g real salt

2 bay leaves

2 large sprigs of fresh thyme

DIRECTIONS

Cut the onions in half through the root, peel them and slice them into thin half-circles. Set the Instant Pot to "Sauté " and add the oil. Once the oil is hot, add the onions. Cook the onions until they have reduced down and become translucent, stirring occasionally to prevent sticking, about 15 minutes.

Add the balsamic vinegar and scrape up any fond from the bottom of the Instant Pot, then add the stock, salt, bay leaves and thyme. Turn off the Instant Pot and close the lid of the Instant Pot, making sure to check that the float is free and the vent isn't blocked and that the lid is set in the "Sealing" position.

Set the Instant Pot to "High Pressure" and cook the soup for 10 minutes once it has come up to pressure. Allow the pressure to release using the "natural release" - don't open the vent or hot liquid may gush out of the vent along with the steam.

Discard the bay leaves and thyme stems, then blend the soup together either using an immersion blender directly in the pot, or by transferring the soup carefully to a blender.

Mexican Beef Stew

Total Time: 40 mins

Servings: 1-2

INGREDIENTS

2 tablespoons fat (or oil)

1 medium-large onion, diced

2 pounds stew meat, thawed

2 teaspoons salt

2 teaspoons cumin

1 teaspoon smoked paprika

1 teaspoon dried oregano

1/2 teaspoon white pepper

1/2 teaspoon chipotle powder

1 cup bone broth

1-15 oz. can fire-roasted tomatoes

1-6 oz. can of diced green chilis

DIRECTIONS

Press the Sauté button on the Instant Pot and add the fat to the pot. Once melted, add the diced onion and sauté 2 to 3 minutes.

Coat the stew meat in all of the spices in a separate bowl. Add seasoned meat to the Instant Pot to sear the meat for 2 to 3 minutes.

Pour in the broth, tomatoes, and green chiles. Place the lid on the Instant Pot, and make sure the vent is closed.

Change the setting to Manual and adjust the time to 30 minutes.

Release the vent when it beeps and allow the pressure and steam to escape.

Oatmeal

Total Time: 10 mins

Servings: 2-3

INGREDIENTS

1 cup steel cut oats

3 cups water

Optional spices

Toppings of your choice

DIRECTIONS

Dump oats into the Instant Pot followed by the water.

Close the lid and close the vent.

Press manual and use the arrow buttons to go down to 3 minutes.

After the oats finish cooling, press the off button or unplug the Instant Pot so the pressure will release naturally.

After the pressure releases, open the lid and give the oatmeal a good stir. It will probably have extra liquid, this will absorb as it cools.

Add cinnamon or other additions and allow to cool slightly before serving.

Top oatmeal with fresh fruit of your choice, apples are shown.

Thai Coconut Chicken Soup

Total Time: 15 mins

Servings: 4

INGREDIENTS

2 tablespoons oil

1 small onion, quartered

2 lbs skinless and boneless chicken breast or chicken thighs, cut into cubes

2 tablespoons Thai red curry paste

1 red bell pepper, cut into strips

6 slices galangal, optional

6 kaffir lime leaves, torn and bruised, optional

3 cups chicken broth

2 tablespoons fish sauce or salt to taste

1 heaping tablespoon sugar

3/4 cup coconut milk

2 1/2 tablespoons lime juice

Cilantro leaves

DIRECTIONS

Turn on the Sauté mode on your Instant Pot.

Add the onion and sauté for 10 seconds before adding the chicken.

Sauté the chicken until the surface turns white.

Add the Thai curry paste, bell peppers, galangal and kaffir lime leaves (if using), stir to mix well.

Add the chicken broth, fish sauce and sugar.

Cover the pot and select High pressure for 10 minutes.

When it beeps, turn to Quick Release.

When the valve drops, remove the lid carefully, add the coconut milk and lime juice to the soup, stir to mix well.

Top with cilantro and serve immediately.

Brown Rice

Total Time: 40 mins

Servings: 1-2

INGREDIENTS

2 cups brown rice

2 1/2 cups water

1 tablespoon extra-virgin olive oil

1 teaspoon kosher salt

DIRECTIONS

Use the sauté setting to heat the olive oil for 2-3 minutes.

Add the rice and stir for 30 seconds. Add water and salt.

Use the manual setting to cook for 22-24 minutes (22 for low elevations, 24 for higher), then allow the pressure to release naturally (don't use the release valve) for 5-10 minutes.

Fluff with a fork.

Chicken Lettuce Wraps

Total Time: 30 mins

Servings: 6

INGREDIENTS

For the chicken:

24 oz. boneless skinless chicken breast

1 celery stalk

1/2 onion, diced

1 clove garlic

16 oz. fat free low sodium chicken broth

1/2 cup hot cayenne pepper sauce

For the wraps:

6 large lettuce leaves, Bibb or Iceberg

1 1/2 cups shredded carrots

2 large celery stalks, cut into 2-inch matchsticks

DIRECTIONS

Combine chicken, onions, celery stalk, garlic and broth (enough to cover your chicken, use water if the can of broth isn't enough) in the Instant Pot. Cover and cook high pressure 15 minutes. Natural release.

Remove the chicken from pot, reserve 1/2 cup broth and discard the rest. Shred the chicken with two forks, return to the pot with the 1/2 cup broth and the hot sauce and sauté 2 to 3 minutes. Makes 3 cups chicken.

To prepare lettuce cups, place 1/2 cup buffalo chicken in each leaf, top with 1/4 cup shredded carrots, celery and dressing of your choice. Wrap up and start eating!

Queso With Cauliflower

Total Time: 10 mins

Servings: 8

INGREDIENTS

For cooking

4 cups cauliflower florets (1 small head of cauliflower)

2 cups water

1 /2cups thick cut carrot coins (3 small carrots)

1/2cup raw cashews

For blending

½ cup nutritional yeast

liquid drained from 2 cans (10 ounce/283 g) RO*TEL diced tomatoes and green chilies

1 teaspoon smoked paprika

1 teaspoon salt (or to taste)

½ teaspoon chili powder

½ teaspoon jalapeno powder, optional

¼ teaspoon mustard powder

Mix-ins

veggies from 2 cans (10 ounce/283 g) RO*TEL diced tomatoes and green chilies

1 Cup chopped bell peppers, optional

¼ cup minced red onions, optional

½ cup minced cilantro

DIRECTIONS

Add the cauliflower, water, carrots and cashews to your Instant Pot and cook on high pressure for 5 minutes, then carefully do a quick pressure release by moving the valve to release the pressure. Or add to a large saucepan and cook on the stove over medium heat until you can pierce the carrots easily with a fork.

Pour the cooked mixture into a strainer over the sink and drain the extra water.

Put the drained mixture along with the nutritional yeast, liquid drained from the canned tomatoes, smoked paprika, salt, chili powder, jalapeno powder, and mustard powder into your blender.

Scrape out the blender contents into mixing bowl and stir in the tomatoes and green chilis and any other veggies you're adding in.

Sweet Potato Chili

Total Time: 15 mins

Servings: 4

INGREDIENTS

Instant Pot or Programmable Pressure Cooker

1 pound of ground turkey

1-2 sweet potatoes peeled and chopped

1/2 medium onion chopped

1 bell pepper

3 celery stalks

1/2 cup crushed tomatoes

1 can black beans, drained

2 cups chicken stock

1 tbsp. minced garlic

1 tsp. cumin

2 chipotle peppers in adobo A sauce

1 tsp. cayenne peppers

DIRECTIONS

Brown ground turkey on sauté function. When you are all done make sure to drain the grease.

Add in the garlic and onions and cook until softened.

Next, mix in cumin and cayenne pepper. Stir in chipotle peppers, black beans, crushed tomatoes, sweet potatoes, and chicken stock. Mix well until everything is combined.

Lock lid into place and turn pressure valve to sealing. Cook on high pressure for 10 minutes using the manual setting. Once the time is up, release pressure using the quick release method.

Remove the lid and switch Instant Pot to sauté. Add in your bell peppers and celery. Let simmer about 5 minutes until the celery is cooked and soft. Turn off Instant Pot and you are ready to serve this tasty dish! Top with cheese, cilantro, and avocado.

Ham and Bean Soup

Total Time: 45 mins

Servings: 10

INGREDIENTS

1 (15 oz) can cannellini beans

1 (15 oz) can kidney beans

1 (28 oz) can crushed tomatoes

1 medium yellow onion, diced

1 cup diced carrots

1 cup diced celery

2 Tbsp Worcestershire sauce

1 bay leaf

1 tsp garlic powder

1 tsp ground mustard

1/2 tsp chili powder

1 tsp kosher salt

1/2 tsp black pepper

Juice from one large lemon

4 cups water

2-3 cups cubed ham

DIRECTIONS

Add all ingredients to Instant Pot. Cover and make sure the valve is on "sealing." Press manual and set the timer to 10 minutes.

Once the timer beeps let the pressure come down naturally for at least 15 minutes.

Carefully release the rest of the pressure and open the pot. Discard the bay leaf.

Season to taste with additional seasonings, if needed. Ladle into bowls and serve.

Store leftovers in an airtight container for up to a week.

You can also freeze this soup in individual containers for a healthy and easy lunch.

Steamed Asparagus

Total Time: 6 mins

Servings: 1-2

INGREDIENTS

Asparagus spears, washed and trimmed (I made 7)

1 cup water

DIRECTIONS

Place trivet in bottom of Instant Pot. Pour 1 cup water in the bottom of the Instant Pot.

Place asparagus across the top of the trivet. If needed, you can cut them in half.

Place the lid on the Instant Pot and turn the valve to "sealing." Press the STEAMING button to 1 minute.

The pressure will build and then the 1-minute countdown will start.

Once the one minute is up turn the valve to "venting." Open the pot and enjoy your asparagus! I serve mine simply with butter and salt and pepper.

Pesto Chicken Rice Soup

Total Time: 42 mins

Servings: 6

INGREDIENTS

3 cups chicken broth (or 3 cups water with chicken bouillon)

2 carrots, sliced into quarter inch rounds

2 ribs of celery, sliced into quarter into pieces

1 medium onion, diced

1 tsp dried oregano

1/2 tsp garlic powder

3 frozen boneless, skinless chicken thighs

3/4 cup brown rice

1 1/2 cups milk or half and half, warmed

1/2 cup basil pesto

DIRECTIONS

Turn Instant Pot to sauté to warm up while you add ingredient to pot. Add broth, carrots, celery, onions, oregano, garlic powder, chicken and brown rice to the Instant Pot.

Secure the lid and turn valve to sealing. Turn off the sauté function, press manual and enter 22 minutes.

Once the 22 minutes is up the Instant Pot will beep. Let it sit for 10 minutes. Then turn the valve to venting. Remove the lid and stir in warmed milk or half and half if you want it creamier. Make sure that it's warmed up or else the soup will curdle. Stir in the pesto.

Ladle into bowl and serve.

Quinoa Porridge

Total Time: 20 mins

Servings: 4

INGREDIENTS

1 cup quinoa, rinsed and drained

2½ cups water

½ teaspoon kosher salt

½ cup almond milk

¼ cup roasted pepitas

¼ cup honey

DIRECTIONS

Combine the quinoa, water, and salt in the Instant Pot. Secure the lid and set the Pressure Release to Sealing. Select the Multigrain setting and set the cooking time for 8 minutes at high pressure.

Let the pressure release naturally for at least 10 minutes, and then move the Pressure Release to Venting to release any remaining steam. Open the pot and stir the porridge to incorporate any extra liquid.

Ladle the porridge into bowls and serve topped with the almond milk, pepitas, and honey, dividing them evenly.

Red Lentil Soup

Total Time: 30 mins

Servings: 4

INGREDIENTS

1 tablespoon olive oil

2 carrots, peeled and diced

2 large celery stalks, diced

1 small yellow onion, diced

¼ teaspoon kosher salt

1 cup red lentils

4 cups water or vegetable broth

1 bay leaf

2 tablespoons fresh lemon juice

Extra-virgin olive oil, for serving

Ground sumac, for serving

DIRECTIONS

Select the Sauté setting on the Instant Pot and heat the olive oil. Add the carrots, celery, onion, and salt, and sauté for about 5 minutes, until the onion has softened and is translucent. Add the lentils, water, and bay leaf, and stir well.

Secure the lid and set the Pressure Release to Sealing. Press the Cancel button to reset the cooking program, then select the Soup/Broth setting and set the cooking time for 15 minutes at high pressure.

Let the pressure release naturally for at least 10 minutes, and then move the Pressure Release to Venting to release any remaining steam. Open the pot and stir in the lemon juice, then taste and adjust the seasoning with salt if needed.

Ladle the soup into bowls, top each serving with a drizzle of extra-virgin olive oil and a sprinkling of sumac, and serve right away.

Pot Roast

Total Time: 1 hr 40 mins

Servings: 8-10

INGREDIENTS

1 (3- to 4-pound) boneless beef chuck roast

salt and pepper

1 tablespoon vegetable oil

1 onion, chopped into big pieces

2 cups beef broth

1 pound of small (1 to 3 inch) yellow potatoes

1 pound of carrots

Lipton onion soup mix

DIRECTIONS

Season roast with salt and pepper. Select sauté and add oil to the cooking pot. When hot, brown roast on all sides, 8 to 10 minutes. Place into the cooking pot.

Add the chopped onions, carrots and potatoes to the pot. Sprinkle on the Lipton onion soup mix and pour on the beef broth.

Select high pressure and set the timer for 80 minutes. When beep sounds, turn off Instant Pot and allow pressure to release naturally for 15 minutes. After 15 minutes, use a quick pressure release to release any remaining pressure.

Carefully remove lid. Transfer potatoes carrots and beef to serving dishes.

If you want gravy, mix cornstarch and water (3t cornstarch with 3t water) and mix in the juices in the pot. Cook while stirring on sauté until thickened.

Made in the USA
San Bernardino, CA
11 December 2017